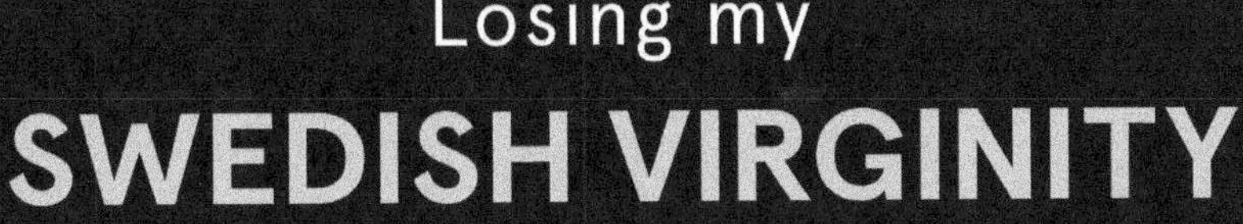

Losing my
SWEDISH VIRGINITY

How to find your way when living abroad

CÉSAR SUÁREZ

SKÖNVIK

Losing My Swedish Virginity

How To Find Your Way When Living Abroad

CÉSAR SUÁREZ

ISBN: 9798561693793

DEDICATION

To my fellow men around the world between 18 and 35 years old.
We are responsible for running the world these days.
We need to become better men.
We need to save the world.
We need to save us.

CONTENTS

Acknowledgments 6

1 An Introduction To My Mind 11

2 Social Media Is A Trap 27

3 Alcohol Is A Risky Business 41

4 Gym Makes You Feel Better 53

5 Young And Human 63

6 Meditation Pays Off 71

7 Healthier Habits 81

8 Quitting News Gets You More Time 97

9 Food And Common Sense Are More Effective Than Medicine 103

10 Business, Education and Women 113

11 Final Statement 129

Epilogue 139

About The Author   143

ACKNOWLEDGMENTS

Thanks to my mom, dad and brother. You are the structure to my life. Thanks to my friends in Lund. You contributed with knowledge and experience. You ignited the brainstorming process that created this book.

LOSING MY SWEDISH VIRGINITY

1. AN INTRODUCTION TO MY MIND

The text you are going to start reading now, I want you to feel as if it were a rap song; extra-long killer lyrics that will give you the vibes to feel better. Great bass, like No Heart-21 Savage-ish mode, with a mix of Wiz Khalifa happy vibes, and some Kanye West's polemic aroma. Jacob told me I should have included a chapter on decisiveness. He said it because I didn't know if I wanted to tell my story along with the tips, or just the tips and the story separate. I decided it is better to have both separate; one as a manual, like a structure of life. The other one more storytelling-ish is a book of poems with the same title as this book, but with a different subtitle and approach. In that one, I write about the crazy lucky and unlucky stuff that has happened to me, since I have been living in Lund, which I transformed into luck. I always felt like this Rich Dad, Poor Dad writer, that I have luck in my life. I have the mindset that I am a lucky person. This introduction chapter may feel a bit disorganized because I wanted to mention a lot about the motivation behind the book and about Sweden before starting with the chapters, but I promise you will get used to my way of writing very soon.

I am living mostly good days in Sweden. Yesterday was one of the good ones. I played football in the morning. We won 10-9, and I scored 9 goals and assisted one. Afterwards, I had lunch with the boys at a very tasty Gambian restaurant in Lund. I was very tired, but I took a cold shower, got myself ready and went to a co-working space where I work every day, including the weekends (so nice when you have the office all to yourself). Then I worked on Xertify (a tech company that I co-founded), sent some emails, did some life admin like paying bills, washing clothes, and dreaming. I went deep trying to close a customer. I contacted them through their website, got friendly with the person behind the online chat and boom, got the phone number of the person I was looking for. Two minutes later, I sent an email introducing our solution and its benefits. Hustle mode on, I went home for dinner, talked about life with my roommates, then back to the office. I stayed until 11:45 pm. My phone died and I did not feel sad or stressed about it. After work, I went to a girl's place, we slept together, and we woke up together. She is ambitious and beautiful, for real. We have been seeing each other for some time now. I am learning the Swedish way of dating. Then, I started my day. Today the sun is spectacular. I have to thank myself and my luck for everything. I stopped for a second and said, "Wow, this is just bloody crazy. This is my life now. I am loving it."

But this book will not be about me telling the stories I have experienced in Scandinavia. Instead, it has more practical stuff, like the books I like to read. I am taking out filters and I am saying things as they are. This book is about self-improvement based on what has been working for me in Sweden. I am writing it before I get famous or I get to an income level in which money doesn't matter anymore. Before my mind gets even more intoxicated, and I get dumb. I am a humble man. I do not plan to change, but who knows. I am already being selective with the people I hang out with. I have read books about these people who are already making it. They write about how to win life from a different position. It can be fun to read that Donald Trump could make his Trump International Golf Links in Scotland, but I just do not have millions of dollars (nor do I owe them like him). It is just another level of whatever you want to call it. I do not even get inspired by it.

We need someone closer to us to talk about life. I have the pleasure to say that I have not made it yet. I am a work in progress. I have at this moment in my bank account, 2,800 USD and about 30,000 SEK; that is all my capital. I am not ultra-rich now. I am not even rich. I may actually be under the Swedish average, for sure (smiley face). But man, I already have 1,100 USD that comes into my bank account every month, and the more I work, the more that comes. I have started to make some money, and I will spend it travelling, investing it on new business ventures, maybe some marketing for this book. But also, on a new company I want to start in Sweden about wellness.

I am currently packing my bags because I am going to Iceland in two weeks. Have you checked the landscapes? The video of Jammie XX DJing in Reykjavik; the video of Justin Bieber "I'll show you" or the blue lagoon? I heard a wealthy and good-looking woman, Swedish CEO of one of the most profitable marketing agencies in Europe saying that before 30, you should save as little as possible. Instead you should enjoy life, meet many people, and definitely travel as much as you can. Afterwards, you may start thinking about adult life; marriage, kids, buying a house, a car or getting depressed. But, before 30, we are all babies. We have muscle and energy. So, it is the time to work hard, travel a lot, and try stuff. Then, when you are in your 50s, you already have the experience, and you know what works for you and what does not. You will have answers to: Where do I want to live? What type of family do I want to have? What type of friends do I like? What is the type of woman that I love? These answers come only by being open to trying new experiences, not even by reading.

With like 2000 USD a month you can manage to have a pretty decent life in Sweden (if it is not Stockholm). Not having financial stress is basic man. After reaching that, you can start creating other illusionary problems in your mind. I feel like I have a pleasant life because I am thankful for where I am, and I am making a supreme effort to do good for the world. Sure, work feels like work (it is a 100x better feeling than financial stress though), but talking with customers, being aware that they are using your product (the one you built with your own hands); feeling that your friends know you and love you; having these calls from mom and dad, from my brother, and a bed to sleep and dream, feels heart-warming. If you work hard, you get more respect. Life is not easy, so taking the easy path will probably only lead to disappointment and unfulfillment.

My dad, a voracious reader, never ever told me life was easy. He always said: "You have to adapt to the circumstances, do not fight against the big current, the world is not fair, get used to it, live with it". Today, I think life is life. It is what it is. No need to categorize it because it is infinite. No need to reduce it, because it is impossible. Being alive, waking up every day is a constant refreshing process. Eckhart Tolle in his book New Earth describes very well the relationship we should have with life. Less ego, more being present, less judgment. I would say it this way: it is important to have a good relationship with the world, but equally essential is to have healthy pockets, a living heart, fulfilling sex and a smart, healthy, open mind.

My idea to write this book came from knowing that there are many people out there in kind of the same situation, with the same worries and limits. When I say limits, I refer 60% of the time to financial limits. You can see me as the same dude you are. I am nothing out of this world. I consider myself handsome, but maybe you are too. I am still an average guy in objective terms, but I am working hard to break it, to get out of the common trap zone. I may get famous with this book. That would be nice actually. But now I am like you. I am a forward-thinking person. I view my life in the long term, and I let myself get amazed by the wonders of planet Earth. These people at the top, they just have more money and more contacts, but in the end they are also full of insecurities and bills. It is better to start at the bottom and make it all the way to the top. Let's just do it (whatever your top means).

One small thing; I did not make this book super long, because I know we all want it quick, to the point, and to have a good time while reading it. A delightful read. Imagine, while you read this that you are at your favorite spot. Maybe at a famous Swedish summer beach like Lomma, with a nice view: people from all ages enjoying the sun, getting that Vitamin D, laughing, talking, playing volleyball, eating ice-cream, living in the moment. What would your perfect beach day look like? Be a creative person. If you can imagine it, you can make it. Or imagine you are reading this, and you are on the rooftop of a building, where your office is located, feeling the fresh air, breathing clean air, and just enjoying the weight of your body in the chair. But wherever it is that you are reading this book, put a good mood to it and to life. But just relax (your mind, not your work), be open and enjoy.

Any triumph that I have accomplished in my life has allowed me to call my mom, my dad and my brother to tell them the good news. I guess that is one of the most powerful fuels you get in your life. I want to cure your weakness and put you back on track, so then you can tell your parents your precious accomplishments. Never the easy way, just pure work.

I wanted a life in which I could hang out with smart people and beautiful girls (and interesting, of course). If a girl is reading this, I bet you want to hang out with the handsome boys too. But also, the smart and honest ones probably! Now I have friends that have podcasts, own summer houses and are funny AF. I am eating good food: sushi, poke bowls, burgers and tasty tacos. Got my cooking skills on point too (Asian cuisine my favorite by far). I am not afraid anymore of buying weird ingredients and following chefs' instructions. Everything you see happening in other people's lives that seems cool, exists, and you can experience it too. Not sure if you want to be the guy who has everything, or the guy that is a friend of the guys who have everything, materially speaking of course. No worries, it's not time to decide. The moment you have those friends you will be a resourceful friend too.

Good life exists and it is expensive. Happiness is expensive. You can pay with money or you can pay with suffering and hard work. Long term goals are achieved through small, everyday progress. If you say you are going to do something, do it. People are scared of people that do what they say they are going to do. You said you were going to read this book. Do it! Do not skip it. And you know man, it is so hard to get out of the loser trap, the poor trap, the lazy trap, and the weak trap. Only the winner mindset people can do it. Only thirsty people can do it. Whenever you escape it, through any door (you have to read The Third Door by Alex Banayan), your life becomes so much easier. The first million is going to be the hardest, always. More honestly, the first 100 bucks you make by yourself without depending on anybody. Those are the sweatiest ones. Then, you make a thousand and boom! If you keep pushing life, good stuff will happen.

I am talking here as if you are my friend. I am being honest here. Life gives us gray days but also bright ones. It is balanced. Nothing can be good all the time. You grow, you lose. It requires a thick skin. Life itself works with a meritocratic structure. The one who works smart, makes it. But also, the one who is open-minded. The one who accepts the mistakes and pushes life also makes it. I am happy that I have felt like trash, so then I can appreciate what victory is. The victories will be small and constant. They will come, I promise.

This book is not for sixty year old people, nor for people that are pursuing careers with Uber as drivers, taking money from the government or cooking for McDonald's. Those are big companies, and if you do that, it should be to learn not to earn, but to get inspired by how big they are, and how they operate. To be fair, The Midas Touch, a book written by Donald Trump and Robert Kiyosaki, has a great point when they mention the cash flow quadrant (smart people get rich by using the money and the work of the other people). Do not get me wrong, I have nothing against people that want an average life or hold a risk-adverse mindset. Maybe you gotta start somewhere. But, I'd rather hang out with people that are forward looking and problem solvers. Less complaining and more doing. I took the time to write this stuff down because it works. It is life changing.

I come from a small city in Colombia. It's called Cucuta. It has an average temperature of 35 degrees Celsius and people there still believe that God will punish you when doing something bad, and at the same time, people, even those scared of God, do those things. They keep believing the words of the same politicians that drain the city; keep watching football in a passionate and depressing way, admiring people for what they have, and not for what they are, and cheating on their partners. Because I was focused since I can remember, I escaped it.

Focused in the way that you do not choose the place where you are born. You happen to start your existence there. Nothing should force you to stay in a place where you cannot grow as you want, or where the population does not share the same values you believe in. I am proud of the things I have done myself, not of the ones I got before I even existed.

I graduated from the best high school in Cucuta (Colegio Calasanz), the best university in Colombia (Universidad de los Andes) and then finished my MSc from the best university in Sweden (Lund University). Now, I am thinking about Harvard or any world top ten university. Why not? I keep working on my projects, educating myself and opening my mind. Before we are 30 (I will probably say before we are 40 when I am thirty-something), we are allowed to go and explore the world. That should be the step zero of every self-development journey; getting out of the place you have been living most of your life. We should have the mindset of being world citizens. I still get the question a lot: so where are you from? I literally do not know what to say sometimes. I have lived in Colombia, Brazil, Portugal, China, the US and Sweden, and I am 25 years old (soon 26). This detachment from any land has allowed me to be freer and travel lighter.

My plan with these tips is to put you in a position in which you can be more confident about being ambitious; about being hungry to get more. I am not promising happiness. I am promising a lot of work. The more work you put on yourself, the closer you get to happiness. I want to be eighty years old and still work on my stuff. I want to be on holiday and catch up on some work that I could not finish during working hours (when you love what you do, why not?). Actually, I am already doing it. I am at the beach taking meetings, feeling productive and enjoying the sun at the same time.

The moment you chill, the other one is working on it double, and once the divergence starts it does not stop. Once people grow, it is very hard to catch them. I am writing in a very honest way here, so, do not be very sensitive. I am willing to receive suggestions about improvements for the book but please read it first. This is a conversation. We are talking next to each other in a living room, and I am saying here what has been working for me. You will see that there is no plan to win in life, but there is only the winner mindset to kill it in life. Attitude matters more than background. In my master's thesis, I found out that people who come from a poor background can get better results in education than people who come from a privileged background, only if they have the beast mindset.

If you have privilege already, you can get even further. You will need to learn the other stuff only people from the bottom know though. Working hard is the best habit one can implement. I say it multiple times so then it can resonate in your mind forever. Discover something worth working for. Loving oneself is also the key; you have to have self love and self respect. Stop sabotaging your life with poor decisions. A person that looks, and hopefully feels it for real, satisfied with his life, is a product of a lot of commitment to himself.

I am going to talk about several topics in the book. All of them relevant in 2020 and probably for the next ten years. I hope you guys enjoy it. I hope to make new friends after writing this book and to inspire you to do your thing. One thing before starting; I do not have a chapter about drug usage, however, smoking weed often is self destructive. Doing other drugs often is not worth it. It is not fun. I have no patience for people that overdo this stuff.

Once in a while, with a chill reason, and whenever you feel happy, maybe it is alright. But man, it is not good for the pocket or the mind. The less harm you do to yourself, the better. You can get high on your own supply by meditating, doing sports or getting good news from your work and studies. There is no need to escape reality. Life is crazy enough itself without making it crazier. Love yourself. If you struggle with drugs, read about it. Take a book about how to quit all of that, and do it. It is worth it. I do not judge. Anyone can do whatever they want, but I do not want drug-addict friends. We all kill it. We all progress in life. If you feel it is a bit out of control, take decisions. It is not good. Grow up. Respect yourself. If you are addicted for any reason, abuse or mental health issues, literally whatever reason, look for help if you cannot deal with it yourself. Life is worth living in real mode, trust me.

I am presenting what has been working for me. People have different needs, and we are usually not at the same stage in life (listen to the song "Stages" from Frank and Walters ft. Cillian Murphy). If you already have a girlfriend that you love and you feel good about it, good for you. That box may be checked already. If you already have your business and want to start a new one, you are probably already aware that it is better to own a company than to work for someone else.

This book is not the Holy Grail for success. It is a very honest, probably immature, view of what every person in their 20s can do to upgrade their life. I am a person that changes constantly, and that is good. We are never the same, and we must not remain the same. A famous author from Colombia, Mario Mendoza, used to say: "Dejese morir, no le de miedo morirse y nacer de nuevo". "Do not be afraid of letting go of the person you were, to embrace the new one". The phase I am in life of self-development has lasted for over 3 years now, and the changes have just been amazing. I broke free from the mediocre and poverty trap. I am no longer depending on my parents' money to survive. I do not discuss here about women and about business in general because I would need a book of 10,000 pages for that (with the main idea to be: work hard). Sleeping with girls is cool, but finding your soulmate is more important. Whenever you spot the right one, she will love you for who you are, not for what you have, to a certain point at least. The goal is not to make her fall in love after she knows all your hustles. She has to love the person that exists deep inside you. It is not easy at all to explain, but love is inexplicable. I cannot wait to talk someday about the girls I have been with, who I have loved for real and with whom I was just not feeling it, even though all seemed to be in place.

This topic and many others in the book are full of contradictions. I may say one thing, and then I may say something different about the same matter. But life is like this; it is important not to put labels on the facts. Life is so random and unexpected. No one knows what they are doing. Fake faces are the easiest to notice. Money matters. Love is awesome, but painful. People are racist, so are you probably, even if you have not noticed it. When you went to the doctor and you said: "oh the doctor is a black man, he must have been very lucky". That is racism. You cure your racism by understanding that the value of people doesn't come from their skin color. We live here in this moment. We are alive. We breathe, we can feel our hands, our head, our legs, and our dicks. We have a body ready to be used to improve the world, while having fun. Some people may say that fighting for a better life seems pointless. I do not agree.

Fighting for a better life is all that I want to do. I cannot stand still and see myself losing days and opportunities. I will take the next boat and discover something new. I am not a ninety-year-old that cannot do anything. I am not bored, nor do I want to be. Much respect for the ninety-year-olds out there by the way. I like recognition; I like people saying I am doing good, that I look good. That is nice. Who does not like that? Why are people so hypocritical in this life? If you do not want to sleep with good looking, educated, fun, open-minded and ambitious girls, that is OK. If you do not want a salary increase, that is OK. I just want to make the point that having a better life is a decision. It takes sacrifice and many failures. No one wins at the first try. But now, before I get madder at people that criticize the ones who dream about a better future, let's start with the social media chapter.

Actually, one last thing. The name of the book "Losing my Swedish Virginity" is because I started a self-development journey before coming to Sweden. I was very anxious, and I found myself going through different panic attacks because I could not exploit my own potential. I felt as if life was already set for me, and I did not like what it looked like. I am not willing to settle for less than I deserve.

A guy like me, from a small city in Colombia, to come to Sweden, to feel confident when surrounded by beautiful Swedish girls, have great business friends and have a professional life here, required some improvements in life. Sweden has many beautiful girls, but they do not sleep with you if you are not tall, blonde, have blue eyes and are basically Swedish (or super confident, funny, relaxed and well dressed). It is hard here to get girls. Every dude is very good-looking, smart and rich, and, Swedish (Ok not all of them, but the point is that the competition is hard, and the standards are high). So for a person to come over and really get the attention of good-looking-smart-educated-ambitious girls, and smart-ambitious-hard-working friends, he needs to take action in his life.

This book is one step closer to that. If it works in Sweden, I promise it works everywhere. Do not judge; I use girls as a proxy. Being good with girls, depending on the quality, i.e. a good-looking girl with an ambitious career who is also pretty, says much about what you can accomplish in life (good communication skills, good hygiene, good grooming, some cash, good friends, fun, ambitious, etc.). By the way, writing this book in Sweden has also made me learn so much about respect and doing the right thing. The more I talk with Swedish people, the more I am amazed by their view on life. I am a young man who came here with an open mind, willing to take as much knowledge as possible in every aspect. I wrote many words of this book that were not right to show to the public. At some points I found myself crossing the limit, using bad words too often, and not feeling good about it. I shared my ideas and got feedback from Swedes (they do live in 2020 regarding integral issues of every society like sustainability, the gender pay gap or mental health). I, by no means, plan to offend anyone, but it can happen. My honesty and my thoughts may have crossed the limit of what makes sense. Again, I was feeling weird and bad about some parts of the book. Until I felt it was right, I didn't share it. I wanted it to be good. Not to release it, and then feel like crap.

Now I know that it was because in Sweden, you actually behave mentally and physically, and you are expected to do a good job, in whatever industry you are in, otherwise you do not feel good. It is like when you go to the supermarket where you have the self-checkout, and there is this supernatural force that makes you pay for every item. I felt the same with this book. There was a supernatural force, something that told me: you do not want this to see the light of day. You need to realize you have to change some stuff, so I did. Accepting that the other person is right is key. When reading this book, try to be like me in Sweden: accept feedback. Just read, be open to the ideas, but do what works for you. It is not that Sweden has no negative points, but man, the culture has developed so much that you learn to behave in society. They are privileged people. I am looking at their culture and their manners from an outsider point of view. Martin, a Swedish friend of mine from Malmö, said: "If you dress like a Swede and you speak Swedish, you are in the society". His words also mean: if you behave as a Swede, you are welcome in the society.

People here have to adapt to strict, sometimes stressful and childish rules. They have high standards; they expect respect and a modern mind. However, I am still authentic. I am still saying what I believe works with pure honesty. The more honest you are with yourself, the more successful you are. The more freedom there is to talk, the more one can move in life. You do not have to waste energy being someone else. In other words, the goal is to be able to be yourself, while maintaining the social conduct of the culture you are in.

I love this country because it is really high quality. They do things so well, and they have good taste. They design cities, buses, cars, health devices, and anything you can imagine, even bags. Anything, and they do it so well that they sell it everywhere in the world. If you come to Sweden and you want to achieve a successful career or be a successful entrepreneur, you need to truly integrate with like top people (business owners, creative minds, innovators, writers, i.e. people with potential to make it big). For that to happen you have to invest in yourself. Networking in the innovation process is as important as capital, knowledge and luck, here and every part of planet Earth. That is what this title is about.

Also, I did lose my Swedish virginity here. It took some time; I had to adjust some lover strategies. But now it does not seem as hard as before. I still see other dudes having a very hard time getting girls here. It is just not easy. The guys who chase the girls or go out looking for girls, are very likely to be the ones that do not get them They are not a prize to be won and the social media platforms literally force you to think about sex all the time. Change the neediness for self-work now. The key is to focus on making yourself better, happier, more relaxed, richer, healthier, and have better friends. I am not trying to put success in these words, and this is by no means trying to reduce the meaning of winning in life. Winning in life is not sleeping with Swedish girls. I would say it is something like, being able to do whatever you want, every day. Like if you want to sleep with a beautiful girl, that will not be a problem. If you want to eat tasty food, that should not be a problem, and be like that with almost everything. I am still young, and I definitely do not have all the answers yet. But I keep educating myself, reading a lot, and having new experiences. Now, I hope you have got yourself comfortable to keep reading.

To finish the introduction, you have to know the structure of the book. It will start with what we should stop. First, the social media trap, then I will present the snare that alcohol consumption is. I transition to the other chapters by presenting our human and young condition. Later, I present the work we need to put on meditation, healthy habits and food. At the end I talk about education, girls and business. For the end, there are no surprising truths that will come up, or maybe it can be surprising for the men that believe that by doing nothing, you get something. This book will be a complement to other authors, that have successfully inspired me, like Anthony Bourdain, Mark Manson, Robert K., Nick Cave and Donald T. (Trump has good books about business, and the guy knows a thing about getting popular, what can you do?), Alex Banayan, Leonard Cohen, Marcel Proust, Jordan Belfort, and Andres Oppenheimer.

2. SOCIAL MEDIA IS A TRAP

Have you received the notification on your phone on a Monday that you have used your phone on average for around 5.5 hours every day for the past week? Boredom is healthy for a creative mind, and using your phone too much kills it.

I have read some papers talking about the problems of social media in people's lives. One of them is from Bilgin and Tas (2018) and it talks about the problems of students at a university in Turkey. It analyzes the relationship between physiological resilience, perceived social support and social media. The thing that the authors of this paper found, from a survey of more than 500 people, was that social media has a negative effect on perceived social support. Social support is described as all kinds of support procured by individuals from others for coping with stressful life events. Social support is an important indicator that an individual is loved, liked, respected and valued. It is the support you have from your family, friends, teachers, neighbors and any other kind of people that can act as a resource to make you feel good. On the other hand, physiological resilience is the ability to recover from difficult moments in your life.

These are things you as a person need to train, and social media is not helping you. The problem is that when something bad happens, you might look for some help from, or some way to fill the void of the problem with, social media. You are allowing time to disappear from your life and just immerse yourself in a digital world of people looking as if they have perfect lives. Nobody has a perfect life 24/7. This is something extremely important that you have to know to start this journey of stopping the bad behaviors and becoming a productive dude or woman.

I think social media should be banned, as cigarettes are for some. In the sense that people with tendencies to feel sad, anxious or depressed are going to be more addicted to social media, and this could become a negative loop of jealousy (you wish you can get the "fun" and "good stuff" others are getting instead of them) and even malevolence. Also, it could make your life look worse than it is. It might be that your life is alright and you will still believe that it is awful. You can't compare pears with apples. RMovies are also fake. TV shows have scripts so you can fantasize about having "x" or "y" life, but that is not real life. You should understand and be aware, that in movies the main characters usually don't show what they do in a period of 24 hours. Which means your life can look as if it is the coolest life ever if you just post the coolest 10 seconds. So that is the point; what you are posting or seeing posted is not anybody's life, it is just social media. You have to understand that this is not real at all. I know you knew it, but we forget it sometimes when we are feeling low or whenever we get distracted by the digital life. This is just a minimal part of someone else's life.

Life is tough, life is not easy. Life is composed of good moments, but also of unsatisfactory moments. Otherwise, please believe that life will be as boring as you could ever have imagined. Yes, and that feeling you have had: the sadness, the depression, the loneliness, the feeling of being extremely bored, the feeling of losing your life, the feeling of wanting to have someone else's life, is caused by social media. It is like with cigarettes; how stupid is it to smoke a cigarette if you know you have a high probability of getting cancer, and then that will kill you? There is no point in doing it. The silly argument of having a bunch of people smoking and not dying doesn't make smoking less bad. There might be some people who are mentally strong and can cope with social media and feel nothing. A number of people are even making money out of it, and are making it a job. Please understand that you are a product on these platforms. Please understand that time is money. Do not keep losing time looking at men or women you would never meet in person. Time is your most valuable asset as Derek (former RSD) says.

Real life is on the streets, not on your phone, not on your screen (which can be broken very easily). Life doesn't get bad easily. Life is beautiful. It is extremely strong and impossible to break into pieces (only in your own small imaginary world if you let it happen). Even when you think so, life is still life man. The best scripts and the best pictures are the ones you have in your mind. Do not worry; those beautiful moments of joy will come if you work for them, by being patient and investing in the long term. If you work like a dog, you are automatically using your phone less. I think people who are wasting time on social media and getting nothing out of it are the dumbest people. Especially if they are aware of what they are doing (they are just unlucky people if they are not). So this is the purpose of these pages: social media is bad and you should quit it. Do not spend even one minute on it. For example, for Instagram, just take your laptop and open their website, go to settings and click on delete account. Do it temporarily if you want to keep your information on their database. But you know, as Charlie Sheen once said about addictions, "You just have to turn it off". You just have to take the decision.

Bear in mind this over-thinking moment of what is your life going to be without social media will make your life shittier. This is false. Starting with the fact that you are going to become more productive. But more productive, not only more productive for work or study, also more productive with your family, friends and lovers. You will start feeling the air, touching the people, and laughing in real life. Once more, all of those experiences, which can be the maximum happiness in life, are not going to come for free. You need to prepare yourself to be the person you want to be. Social media is not the way. Forget it; it will only make you feel uglier and poorer. And as Michael Caine used to say, "You would always find someone who is more beautiful, more talented, more funny and so on, and so forth in life". So, stop comparing yourself and put an end to trying to make a sad statement out of it, like: what am I gonna do without it? (sad face). Life is beautiful as it is. Enjoy your family, friends and time. Do whatever you want, just do not be weird. And guess what, knowing how to act as a normal person in life is only learnable by doing it. You learn how to talk to a girl by doing it. Most of the most amazing things in life you have to live yourself. Do not let anyone tell you the stories. Do not worry, while exerting oneself, a time and a place will create an opportunity for you. Only you have to make sure you're prepared to face the moment.

Some people say: you should go out and meet people. Well, we all know that is not easy at all. Like, show me first how you are doing it, and then I will tell you if I admire you or not. The thing is that, as in everything, luck plays an important role in all you do. So if you did quit social media and you are thinking about what to do with your life now, I have some good tips for you. First of all, set a goal. It can be a big one, a medium one or a small one. Try to see where you want to be in three months time and then set small steps to accomplish those goals. Keep your head up and maintain optimism. Sometimes you will feel extremely bored; you will feel you should be doing something else with your life and you are not doing it. But please, do not rely on this problem on not having someone to do the things you like with. Before you get a new friend or a new girlfriend/boyfriend you should have a stable life.

If you are just waiting for a miracle to happen to you, let me tell you, it will not come. Do not expect to meet someone at the library, fall in love and create a family. You have to do stuff to achieve that. Nothing is for free. Life is full of people willing to work for their dreams. Those people are the ones that can achieve things. They (us if you get serious about self-improvement) will be the people men dream about being in the future. But as this chapter refers to social media, quitting social media is one fabulous step towards becoming not the consumer of content, but the producer of it. Social media is terrible. I have to repeat it in order to make it powerful and real. Social media is a waste of time. It is better without it than with it. No more sabotaging yourself.

So as promised, here are the activities I recommend doing instead of being on social media. You can do all of them as many times as you want.

Read interesting books. By interesting, I mean books that you will put into practice in the next few months. Do not read random topics about random people. That is just as bad as Netflix. You have to read books connected to the person you want to be. If you want to be a good economist, then buy an economics book. Life is simple. If you want to be a master of seduction, then buy a book teaching you how to be a master of seduction and apply this with everything. But be careful; remember that books can only teach you codified knowledge and that for you to learn the complete thing, you have to learn the tacit knowledge. And what I mean by this is that, as my teacher used to say, if you and me both have the same recipe to prepare a tasty chili con carne, your dish and my dish would probably be different. This is because we both have the codified knowledge, which is the recipe, but we have different tacit knowledge on how to use this knowledge. Therefore, it is important to put the things you learn into practice. At that point you can learn for real, and you are not just wasting time in your life. Because for you to know, life has a time limit and it goes freaking quickly.

Go out for walks on the street, or in parks. One of the best things you can do is to just go out and walk to see new people, to breathe fresh air and to move your legs. You might think this is only for old people, and that you might look weird doing it. But as some other people say: you stop doing things in your twenties because you worry about what others say, then when you are in your forties you might start doing things because you don't care about what other people think, and then when you get even older you see that people in fact never cared about you. This is the thing with morning walks. In your mind, it might seem awkward to see a young dude or a young adult trying to be mentally healthy and physically active. But for your information, nobody gives a damn about what you are doing (if you are not disturbing them). So go for a walk, do some walking meditation. Feel every step while you walk. Watch your thoughts. Create new companies and dream about them. Try to say hello to people while you walk. Look for eye contact. Try to smile at people. Feel that you are alive. Just do it. Just feel life.

Have a morning routine (it is so important). Instead of waking up and using your phone for social media distractions. Just take a big glass of water and drink it. Just get out of bed. Feel you are ready to face the day. Make the day memorable. Be thankful for waking up. Be aware that you are alive. Be aware that you have people thinking about you. Yes, you do. I recommend here some short mindfulness. Like a couple of deep breaths, opening the curtains, waking up with the rhythm of a good song. Then if you eat eggs, cook them. If you buy the ones that are EKO, i.e. fulfill ecological and ethical standards, they will taste finer. For a small price difference, you can eat healthier and support better treatment of the chickens. I usually put the eggs with ham and cheese, or with some veggies or whatever, and then, I leave the eggs cooking and go to the shower. My best tip here is to only take cold showers, and the reasons I will explain later on. But also, you can start with warm water, and then when you feel ready, just decrease the temperature of the water gradually until you reach a point where the water cannot go any colder. You will feel extremely ready for the day even if you want to or not.

Afterwards, get dressed and finish your breakfast. Have a good warm coffee afterwards and eat some fruit. I quit coffee actually. I get so anxious, especially in the winter. So I am going through a phase without caffeine. I am having tea instead. But you do you.   A morning routine is basic; it keeps you busy, but productive, and puts you in the right mood to start the day. The perfect morning routine might be different for you. Just have one. Something you enjoy doing every day. And if you do not know what you enjoy every day for a morning routine, then just try new things until you want to repeat them. For me, the cold showers were something I tried, and I kept it. But for example, doing yoga in the morning after waking up was not my thing. I just tried it but did not do it anymore. Also, reading the news I thought was something I really enjoyed, but not anymore. Actually, your morning routine is an evolutionary process, a dynamic one. It might change but it has the structure that makes you feel comfortable. Just try new things and keep the ones you enjoy and take out the ones you don't. Also, remember that you do not have to punish yourself if you cannot do your morning routine. Whether it happens, it doesn't matter; sometimes we just don't have the time or we just don't feel in the right mood. It is normal because we are humans and we are far from being perfect all the time.

You see, that is the thing with social media. We become digital creatures that don't feel 98% of the normal emotions a normal person in the real life feels. We are humans, so, it is alright to feel distressed some mornings and to skip 80% of the morning routine, or just skip it all because you have no time. It doesn't matter. Don't feel bad for it. The next day you can take it again and come back to the things that make you feel strong and comfortable in the morning.

When at a party or any social gathering, put away your phone. Imagine being in a techno club when the DJ has the best set and you just want to keep posting videos, or whatever, to show others what you are doing. Remember that no one cares about what you are doing. It doesn't define you as cool or not. The action of putting it on social media is just saying, probably like yelling, that you want some attention because you are not having enough fun in real life. Now, imagine the person looking at that post of yours on their phone. That person would probably think: this person is not smart enough to enjoy life properly; this person is bored at that place; this person wants to tackle someone specifically to get attention; or this person is actually having fun. If it is the last one, the person watching your post will very likely not feel so good. They will feel the same way you feel when seeing other people's posts. It is just so much nonsense. It is even trashy to write about it, trying to describe the moment. It just seems so pointless. So then, what are you doing? Just be there in the present moment, and enjoy that DJ's set, or that jazz band. Or if you are at a house party, what a terrible way not to be present is to keep posting on social media while you are there. Imagine it is the same as when your family used to say to you: put your phone away when eating. Come on! It is the same bro. Do not do it. It is just a matter of saying no.

I do not want to waste my time and life on imaginary worlds. I want to live in the moment, I want to be present. I want to meet new people, or if there is someone in the room that I already know, then I want to talk about topics I do not know that they might know. Just ask questions about anything that comes to your mind. You will get inspired if it is a cute girl. So to end this point, if you are at a party just put your phone away and enjoy the moment. If it is horrible without a phone, then just go home. You are not by any way forced to stay where you don't want to be. It is easy, life is not that complicated.

I know it is extremely hard to put the phone away when you are at school and the class is boring, but it is something you have to do. Firstly, to show respect to your classmates, and to the teacher. Just think that it is cooler to pay attention to the teacher than to look at your phone. I mean, I am talking about social media. But if you are having a nice text session with the love of your life, this of course is more important. Just be prudent. Know what you are doing. Is it worth it? You are the only one who can tell if the thing you are doing on your phone is in fact more relevant than the class. I have the answer if you think Instagram is more important. But I don't have them if you are reading New Yorker articles, learning about something you might use in a real life interaction. Just be honest with yourself. But take it easy, don't overcomplicate anything. You do what feels right to do. Don't be too strict with yourself.

Remember to be comfortable and happy with your decisions, but always try to look for things that are going to be good for you in the present, and in the future. For example, reading that article about artificial intelligence in a science magazine might work for talking with your friends or coworkers, or whoever. But, looking at some hot chick pics on Instagram may not, because it is an easy thing to do. Anyone, even the dumbest person in the world can do it.

I am aware that you have YouTube, LinkedIn, Instagram, Facebook and so on. It is hard to disconnect from the world. You actually do not need to cut it off as it will probably create more anxiety, but take some detox periods. **Go offline for two months at least.** Feel how you feel without it. Enjoy it, it is worth it. Just have Facebook messenger and delete the app. Also, turn off all notifications on your phone. It is good not to be a slave to your phone. Some people also recommend putting the screen on black and white mode to enjoy the action of watching the screen less. But man, the truth is that you will likely not quit social media. So relax, it is not a big deal, just use it less and if you can, do not use it at all. But please bro, you probably already know it, but I will say again: social media sucks because it is bad for your mental health. If you are not making money, or getting laid out of it, then it is probably better not to use it. People who do care about you will have your number. Instagram is the one I hate the most. It is the evil himself (God, in this scenario, will be like having some friends over and cooking with them). But do not let this evil take your soul.

After a while you know that all of these hot chicks do not seem that hot anymore. The level of satisfaction you get from watching these pics has decreased over time. It is like that. Do you like that? Real life girls are not Instagrammers. In fact, the famous ones on Instagram are humans too (bad breath sometimes, insecurities, dreams, hopes, problems, family, friends, etc.). So, do yourself a favor and stop it. If you have a girl that you are seeing, or you want to, take it to SMS or to Whatsapp ASAP. Otherwise, every time you talk to her you will have to check Instagram.

For LinkedIn, I have to say it is a kind of useful type of social media. You need to post your thoughts and keep bragging about your work-related achievements. It also sucks because no one posts that they lost their job. They do it sometimes, with the aim of getting emotional support from other people. I guess that less than 1% are like, oh you lost your job, here have a new one. It can happen, but it is not likely. LinkedIn is good for maintaining your professional network; good to have sales contacts and to make professional contacts. But you can also find beasts out there. Do not trust the profiles of the people. Do not reveal information about your business, or your ideas, or your opinions for free. It has happened to me that low quality dudes want to have a chat with me, and take my ideas for free.

So, please, be careful on the internet in general. Same with girls, same with everything. Life cannot be more digital than real. You gotta make a life outside of your digital world. Do not lose a full day on the screen doing nothing. Yes, feel bad for yourself but do something about it. I could have written infinite options of things to do instead of being on social media, but it is literally anything you can do in the real world. The one I like the most, of the ones I mentioned, is to read. Read many books and you will see how you easily get the smart-beast mode you need to hack life, and enjoy it as much as possible.

To be honest, I still use Snapchat to talk to girls. Instagram a couple of times every week to add the new people I meet, but quickly after I move them to Whatsapp or SMS. It gets so much better. LinkedIn, for professional work as I mentioned; Facebook, for planning some football games and chatting with people in general (on my laptop I have the news feed eradicator that puts motivational quotes). I do not know what they do with the data but I mean, they are eradicating your feed so it is good. Also, on Facebook I have a group for the Wim Hoff Method, and some posts of paintings of the 18th and 19th century. I am not posting anything there. Regarding Tinder, I got out of control for several months. I was using it, getting addicted to it, and literally not going on any dates. I use it a maximum of 15 minutes a day with the option of the iPhone to limit your time on apps. Tinder has to be used for sending your texts and fixing dates. No more than that, and also move the people as soon as possible to other less time consuming apps like Facebook Messenger or SMS. Whenever you feel you are losing control of it, getting super excited about it, getting super happy when someone texts you, or matches with you, that is a sign.

In general, I detox during the winter and during the summer I use it more. I am not perfect. I wish I was not using any of those, but it is so necessary in this tech world we live in, that you are kind of forced to. It is good to keep it healthy. Do not envy anyone; work to get your own stuff. Do not get distracted; most social media things are fake. I cannot stress enough how important it is not to use social media. But hopefully you got my point by now. Do not use it, or at least, decrease its use considerably (and have some detox periods).

References:

Bilgin, O. and Tas, I. (2018) 'Effects of Perceived Social Support and Psychological Resilience on Social Media Addiction among University

Students', Universal Journal of Educational Research, 6(4), pp. 751–758. Available at: https://search.ebscohost.com/login.aspx?direct=true&db=eric&AN=EJ1175375&site=eds-live&scope=site (Accessed: 2 November 2020).

3. ALCOHOL IS A RISKY BUSINESS

The truth is that alcohol is pretty bad for mental and physical health. When you are young and beautiful, it feels fine to drink alcohol to enjoy life. It seems fine to be drinking every weekend and to have a budget for alcohol, equal to or even higher, than that for food. It also seems fine to assume it is a normal thing to be intoxicated and to know that the next day you might feel like crap. Alcohol intake also induces you to make bad decisions or decisions that you would never have taken if you were not drunk. These decisions can be a range of very stupid decisions like having sex without a condom, getting into a stupid fight, or acting like a clown in front of people that know you, and that are going to see you sober the next day. You can think also about the positive effects of drinking: it makes you more sociable, it makes you cooler, it makes you feel you are part of the group, and it definitely makes you feel more confident to do anything. I am not saying alcohol cannot bring good things. But definitely anything you can do with alcohol, you could have done without alcohol. Even talking to that pretty girl you like, even that. And maybe you would have been playing a better game with her.

Just for a moment, imagine those happy mornings when you are alone and dancing to the best beat, the one that feels freaking good (for instance, "Sorry" by Justin Bieber. What? I like it though). A good song puts you in an awesome mood to enjoy life. It puts you in the mood to send a cute message to the girl you just matched on Tinder. These same feelings are the ones you try to look for when you are planning to drink. Just think about the feeling of being full of energy, versus the feeling of being hungover. Just think about the benefit to your personal finances if you do not include alcohol as an expense anymore. Some people want to change their life for the better, but they are not willing to take the risk. When you win something you also lose something. It is like when you move from one city to another; you might miss your previous group of friends and the food, but you will also find new friends and new tasty food. Then, just do not be afraid of taking the decision of going sober. It might be one of the best decisions you can ever take to improving your wellbeing.

Quitting alcohol is an individual decision in which the group of people around you, your family and your friends, have a strong influence. Some people are just passive drinkers. They just drink because their family or friends drink. They don't even like to drink. I was like that, I can say. I really didn't enjoy drinking for the last few months before going through a sober period. I didn't enjoy it at all. I just did it because it felt socially right to do it. But how can we be so simple-minded by harming ourselves, and our finances with alcohol? Nobody will feel the hangover for you. Therefore, the best way to fight the hangovers is just not to drink at all.

I can make a list of all the things you could buy if you accept reducing your alcohol intake to very minimum levels, or even to zero. There might not be any safe level of drinking. And this thing again, thinking that you are young and invincible, and that you would never ever get a disease related to alcohol consumption, is just a huge lie. You can easily die from drinking alcohol. It is true you don't need to be in your sixties to feel the negative problems that drinking has. Every time the next day comes, you can just feel it by yourself.

I used to think before that people who don't drink are just square and all they want is to kill the party or the vibe because they cannot drink. But now I think these people can be awesome and inspirational. Not drinking can be way cooler than drinking. It shows respect for your body and mind. It shows that you have principles, and that you are mentally strong enough to say NO to drink, even when there is social pressure. Every time you think you cannot enjoy a party because you are not drinking, just remember you are coming back to a memory that is in the past. The present is always yours. You have a blank page every day to make better decisions in your life. You would feel awesome being full of energy on Saturdays and Sundays, while everybody else is feeling like shit. But please, also remember not to be a dick, or presume that you are a more valuable person because you took the decision to not drink. Don't make it like vegans. Just take the decision and keep it. Hold it, and feed it. Try to go sober for the next parties. Put some challenges and quit gradually.

The beast mode would be to start your next day saying: I am not going to drink anymore, boom! Just turn the drinking off. It is not easy, but for sure it would help you to have better routines on the weekends and a way healthier lifestyle. Better at sex, better at the gym, better sleep, better mood and also more money in your pocket. I just think it is for stupid people to not change for the better. Then you really don't deserve the good things that are coming because of the change. Try to be mature, even if you feel you are not. Try new things and keep the new ones you like. Of course, you can drink water or alcohol-free beverages like zero percent beer or wine. You can still be holding a cup or a glass of something and laugh with your friends. Just remember when you were on holiday from high school: sober and still having a blast with your friends. You can keep the good and remove the negative-bad. You can do it. Look always forward. Be today the man you want to be tomorrow. Do not wait a second to make an improvement in life. Everyone will see you as a smart person who takes care of himself.

Just be prepared to face the challenge. Just write down why you want to stop drinking and keep track of the sober days. Keep track of the positive things you think quitting alcohol is bringing, and of course you can also write down the negative effects of doing it. Do not worry, any problem you encounter, you will find a way to face it and convert it into a beautiful thing for your life. Just as an example, think about when you will be a grandfather talking to your grandchildren in a very positive vibe and honest way, about the reasons you joined the cool movement of quitting alcohol. If we as a society are always improving, and we are capable of overcoming any negative effects of change, we as a society can become a non-drinking one. No drinking (smiley face) and (sad face) if you do it. But always remember not to be rude with yourself, i.e. don't hate yourself or draw general negative conclusions about yourself based on a specific situation. You are human, you can drink sometimes, just chilling, you don't need to be super strict, just enjoy. You just need to know that you are harming yourself every time you drink and that is not a smart decision. The more you drink, the greater the harm. A couple of beers with the boys is nice, but man, there is no need to get shit-faced.

If reading this does not convince you to quit alcohol, I am going to mention more life facts:

I play soccer with a football team in Sweden, and one of the mates that plays with me looks very healthy in the mind, and bodywise too. I became curious because he always gives an extraordinary performance in training and during games. I asked once how his weekend was and he just said: "It was good, with my girlfriend". Then I asked if he usually goes to parties and gets smashed. He answered: "If I drink even a couple of beers I can feel that my performance for training and games is going to decrease, therefore, I just try to not do it". He also said he only drinks a couple of times per year in very low amounts. People who have a partner drink way less than people who don't. I have seen from my personal experience, how single people want to get drunk in order to fill that void of not having someone. They usually end up having sex with undesired partners and regretting bad decisions from the night before. I am only generalizing to make it more dramatic.

Drinking alcohol puts you in a very bad mood. No matter how hard you try, it is just a terrible mood that we feel afterwards. Of all the nights I have been drinking, there is not even one that I remember saying: I am very happy to have this hangover. This never happens. Even if you wake up next to a hot girl. Even if during the night something awesome happened. Hangovers are always crap.

Nobody likes drunk people. When you go out and don't drink anything you can feel this superior feeling of being the smartest person in the room. You will see most people having problems walking or dancing. Even problems speaking. Even very unpredictable behavior You will feel like an outsider. At the beginning it can be a strange feeling, but it gets comfy with time.

You talk a lot of shit when you are drunk, and this is regrettable. All of the things you are not able to say when sober are better not said when you are drunk. If those are feelings-related, just think again. Those feelings are with you all the time; those feelings were not created because you drank. Therefore, you have to be a man able to talk about your feelings, even when you are not drunk. You feel so much lighter when you show people what you feel. And it is amazing when you do it with a clear mind. It is like with meditation: if meditation is awesome when you have a cloudy mind, meditation is ten times more awesome with a happy and clear mind. It is the same. You just don't need to be fucked up to talk.

Alcohol consumption takes days from your life every time you are hungover. Be honest, when you are hungover you do not want to do anything. You even lose the whole day because you have no energy, and only bad thoughts come to your mind. Even if you meet some friends for brunch, or even if you are going to meet family for a huge meal, you will feel below par afterwards. The hangover only starts when the next day is ending. When you wake up, you are still drunk. Just give it a couple of hours and you will know how much you drank last night.

I really get pissed off about the alcohol business. I really hate that they promote the biggest events in the world. That it is legal to show marketing that is targeting all kinds of ages. I wish drinking was a bit more taboo. In Sweden, every alcohol marketing campaign has the same labels as the cigarette packages. I hate thinking about companies that are making money by making me more stupid and destroying my life. Because this is what I feel when I drink too much: that my life is shit, there is no other way to call it. This shitty feeling of feeling shit. I am not going to pay any company to make me feel like shit. I am not that stupid. The system will not tell me how to conduct my weekends or how to celebrate a birthday. The freedom to do evil marketing by these huge monopolistic alcohol companies is just very, very sad for our society. In the world cup, in the UEFA Champions League, at your favorite concert, in the middle of the news, when reading any article on the internet, everywhere man.

Another very terrible fact, is the will to pee everywhere. Would you like to get rid of that dying feeling of waiting in a line to go to the toilet? For your information, if you drink beer like it is water, your chances of having this problem in your life will increase too. I hate this feeling, it is horrifying. I am very impatient, so I just pee anywhere, which is extremely bad according to the law and social norms. Peeing where you shouldn't pee is a terrible and regrettable action. You can get rid of this.

Alcohol consumption creates a dependency on you for the night. You usually wait until the alcohol kicks in a bit in order to start having fun. What a dumb thing this is. You, again, don't have any fun until you are a bit drunk. Then, you are waiting for something, like your brain is thinking about the alcohol. It is more work for your brain (which could have been used on a strategy to have more fun, or just to be more present in the conversation you are having). You don't have to wait for the alcohol kick to be who you are. This is not an alpha thing to do. Only people with low confidence do this and it is bad. It creates dependency, i.e. it makes your brain believe that you need the alcohol. You don't need it. You are cooler by not being drunk. It is extremely hard to control the social part of the drinking. I am aware of the fun in drinking. But the point is to love yourself more than the group of people you are with. It is not easy, it takes sacrifice, but it is completely worth it.

Everyone wants to quit drinking after drinking, but almost nobody does it. This happens because we are taking the easy step. The easy step will always take us to the same places. We want to have better weekends and a better life, but we do nothing to improve. We don't dare change our negative actions because we are weak. We are humans, and it is not a big thing to be weak. But we can prepare ourselves and fight the corrupt, easy way of solving things. If we want change, we need to make it. We cannot wait until something terrible happens because of drinking. We certainly don't want that. We might want to be forced to put some pressure to make us change, but this is more painful. A death? No thank you. I'd rather do it myself. I'd rather fight against the demons in my head that make me make stupid decisions, than wait for something terrible to happen. Because alcohol is also there when something terrible happens, and by no way can it be a solution. It is not. Being a man means being able to respond like a man in any situation in life. Don't be a baby. You can cry all the tears you want to, but it takes courage to quit drinking. Cry all you want, but if nothing is changing it is because you are crying more than doing. You are the only one who can solve your problems.

Another very awesome fact which puts you in a good mood for not getting drunk, is that very rich and successful people don't use it. And don't think they are having less fun because they are not using it. They are having more fun and they are making more money than us (poor-alcohol-dependent-people). They also have better girlfriends. In this case, a good girl is the one that makes your sleep, diet, productivity and energy better. So, they sleep better. And for sure they make better decisions in life. One example is a very good friend of mine from Colombia, Jose, who is extremely good with business. Extremely good, extremely organized and he has the girl of his dreams next to him. He doesn't have time to waste on negative and toxic stuff, he just goes for the things that add value to his life. Awesome friend. The more I think about him, the more I respect and appreciate his friendship.

Making hard decisions might be very difficult because they put a lot of stress on you. Therefore, you don't need to quit completely if you really don't want to quit. If you decrease your alcohol consumption for a certain period, and over time you are less dependent on alcohol to have fun, it is alright. It is a win. We live in this cultural bubble so hard to get out of, that it is totally understandable. Also, if you have a really good moment and you feel it is right to drink at that moment and at that place, just do it. We are not alive to be perfect. We just set some standards and we adapt ourselves according to the different moments in life. Even though we have to have in mind that alcohol is bad for us and it is necessary to get rid of it in our life, if you are with the love of your life and everything is going great and she suddenly appears with a bottle of wine, you are not going to say no. You get my point? Just be smart enough to always make better decisions. The most important lesson here of this chapter is that you have to be aware that alcohol is bad for you. It is up to you if you want to let it control your life. If you are making any decisions which take into account all of these bad qualities of drinking and you still think the pros are bigger than the cons, then do it. But if you are going to drink just don't abuse it. Just do it a little for very special moments. Just go with the flow of learning and leaving it. Enjoy the healthy melody of sounds from your mind saying thank you for taking care of me.

Don't over think about not drinking. Don't count the beers. Don't count the number of people getting drunk. Try to not compare yourself. Just train your excuse for not drinking. If some of your friends ask you to go for a beer and you say: yes I'll go but I won't drink, don't feel bad for it. It is you taking a decision to improve your life. Or, order an alcohol-free beer, or order one, and make it last.

Try to go to the gym while having a hangover. Try to go to class while having a hangover. Try to drive while having a hangover. Try to have a serious meeting while being hungover. Try to run while being hungover. Try to sleep while having a hangover. Try to watch a movie while being hungover. Try to feel happy while being hungover. I can go for infinite things to do and for sure all of them are better to do while not being hungover. The real name for which must be: to be intoxicated and sick.

Drinking sucks. Especially when you feel low, and you drink to be more present. I used to drink to destroy the social anxiety of going to parties with random people. I literally needed a beer or two, otherwise, I'd feel like I was getting a panic attack on the dance floor. So much anxiety. The solution of drinking was also causing me more anxiety. Alcohol can help you get you laid, sure, but do you like having sex while being drunk? My point is that all of this can happen without being drunk. If you are just not getting drunk often, and if you are not drinking often, you are fine. This chapter goes more to the people that do not have control over their drinking. Like drinking every day, what is that bro? Only losers do that; only people that do not like themselves. Alcohol is cool for dinner, some wine, and then some fine conversation. That is a cool plan. It is not cool to drink 15 beers and go to bed completely smashed without a wallet and alone.

I still drink wine at dinner with friends. I like the plan of having dinner and drinking wine. It is just so nice. But the plan of getting drunk-smashed with the boys, I am not doing it anymore. The plan of going stupid until 8:00 AM and then wasting one day of my life because of the hangover, no thanks. You grow up. You have to experience the downside of alcohol to see how bad it is (you can also trust me on my word). Please, drink less. Do it, and the next day you will be able to do your tasks. A night out does not need to mean losing the next day because of a hangover.

One trick I did myself was going from 15 beers a night, to 5. Then, I stopped drinking beer and bought expensive whiskey. Then, I drank only small sips of whiskey. A bottle could last for like a month. Less hangover, more boss feeling and more relaxed. The thing about everything is about trying new things. Are you not tired of drinking the same low quality beer? Try some cocktails. Just move on, grow up. I do not want to sound like I'm promoting alcohol consumption. I am promoting a healthy way of doing alcohol. I hate strict people, they suck. I know I said before it is good if you quit it completely, but I still know that drinking moderately is fine. So do it, do not feel bad about doing it. Man, life is so short and so beautiful, that drinking a fucking glass of wine is completely worth it. Just do it lagom. Swedish people are not good at it. Do not be like some Swedish people that need to get smashed to get their feelings and joy out their bodies. It is disgusting. Be chill, never drunk, never stupid, always happy, always having fun. "Having fun" does not mean getting smashed.

I have much respect for addictions. I have respect for people who depend on alcohol to do stuff. But bro, we are able to enjoy life without being drunk. We can do it. No more narrow-minded beliefs Try a sober life. Going through some sober periods helps too. Doing outdoors activities, going to the gym, etc. The funny thing is that parties are not the only way to have fun (and not the only way to meet girls). We live in this bubble of crap in which it seems that there are limited plans we can do. Well, that is just not true

4. GYM MAKES YOU FEEL BETTER

My take on going to the gym will be very simple: the body gets stronger, so does the mind. Because when you think you are not able to do one more rep, you do it. You think you can´t manage a certain situation, but it happens that you can even go for more. The perfect routine for going to the gym starts at any time of the day. There is the saying that if you go in the morning, you will have better sleep at night, and if you go at night, you will have calmer mornings, but it really isn't that strict. You can go to the gym anytime you want. Actually, sometimes you will not feel like going. Just watch a video of Jocko Willink: "Out, now!", and you will have an ex marine yelling at you for being a lazy bastard.

For me, the feeling of going to the gym is superior. Before having the habit of going to the gym, I usually played football to think about other stuff not related to my stressful life. It was awesome playing football. I enjoyed it a lot. But it is different, very different. Playing football does not count as leg day. Before going to the routine and tips, I want to make one thing clear: you should have liberation from your daily course in life. The modern life created by evolution and the intelligence of humans, negatively affects the mind and the body. Therefore, you need to escape and use the body that you have, as if we were in very olden times. Otherwise, it would become completely obsolete. It would cause osteoporosis, back pain, leg pain and hundreds of other sedentary-people diseases.

So, if you don't like the gym, but you like yoga, do yoga. Yoga should be as equally important as going to the gym because you really need to improve your flexibility. I am lazier to do yoga, than to go to the gym. However, whenever I exercise, I stretch beforehand and afterwards, and the next day, I feel like I'm 15 years old. For you to know, Indian people say that flexibility is more important for the mind and body, than building muscle. So yes, if you have the chance to do yoga with going to the gym, and then some sport you really like, like tennis or squash or football, you have the perfect combo. Then for sure, no doubt, you will stay healthy and motivated throughout the week.

Let's say you are hungover, and you want to do a workout at the gym. No way. Don't do it (re-read the previous chapter). I don't recommend it. It's better to not be hungover when going to the gym. If you feel hungover, have a cold shower, eat good food, rest and drink tons of water. But if you have paid attention to what I just mentioned about alcohol, you might not have a killer hangover anymore.

Coming back to the gym, you need to be patient. It takes at least three months to start seeing results, but this is an awesome feeling. When people start telling you: oh man, you look bigger! Oh man, you look good! It is a good feeling. It is the feeling of being congratulated for your hard work and your consistency. It is the feeling of getting something that there is no other way to achieve than with some weights, and a lot of effort at the gym. I remember reading some old literature, I do not recall the book, but someone defines happiness as the moment people start recognizing your work. It is a great feeling, I love it. It is something you did right, and something that is worth sharing.

It is worth wearing clothes that allow you to look more handsome, i.e. to show those gains without shame. That is another part of the benefits. You can just feel the confidence of having a good body. Remember though, that a beautiful face or a beautiful body means nothing, compared with attitude and intelligence. So don't think you will have life easier just because you are going to the gym. No way. But it would feel good, no doubt.

To go to the gym, I recommend eating very well before and afterwards. I am not the kind of person who is very strict with food and has to weigh it, no way. Just eat a lot (I do not know very well how it works when you want to lose fat!). If it is in the morning, three or four eggs with ham and cheese, with onions and tomatoes, bacon, or with whatever you want to put with the eggs, is an awesome start for breakfast. The bacon part may sound very unhealthy, but it is kind of tasty. If you have a healthier way, go for it. You can have some bread, some lemon juice, a banana and then some coffee (or tea). For me, this is a winner's breakfast (you will notice it many more times in the book). Of course, after eating this you have to wait at least an hour and a half to let your body digest, or three according to Lionel, a French chef that is a friend of mine. But you will feel the beauty of the food power once you are at the gym.

When you are there you will be lifting weights, and you will think that you are going to faint because there is too much energy you are putting on the weights. Relax, you will know that this will not happen because you had such a great breakfast/meal. Of course, don't be extreme. Just a reasonable effort won't make you faint. You can consume other kinds of food, but be aware of making sure to have a variety of protein and vitamins in your stomach. I really don't recommend using any kind of laboratory-made products like energizers, creatine…etc. It costs way more money than this beautiful breakfast, and is not natural. If you are vegan, you will know how you can replace the eggs with other stuff. The main idea is to go to the gym with your stomach in a good mood.

Usually, as I have to wait for my food to digest before going to the gym, and for the caffeine kick or for whatever reason after eating breakfast, I take time to make the decisions of the day and to see what the outcome is that I expect from the day. I don't leave any decisions for later, and if I think I didn't make the right ones, then I will make the one I took, the right one. For example, one day I got a date on Tinder but I had to go to Copenhagen, without knowing how the encounter was going to be. I just woke up quite stressed because I didn't know if it was worth going to Copenhagen, which was like 45 minutes by train and some $30 bucks away. I said, I am not going to think about it, I am just not going to go. Of course, a couple of hours later my mind came to ask me why, why, why, why? Like a million times. So I just focused my day on making it the right decision. This in part, by doing a very good routine at the gym (the gym works whenever you need to compensate for what you thought screwed your day, or that it was not a good one). Eating very good food through the day, and doing the other stuff I had planned to do.

So if you see, the decision doesn't matter, but how you make it the best one. Also, if I had chosen to go on the date I would have made it a very enjoyable one. But as it is not the case, I don't even try to think about what would happen with that. So coming back to the point, the time you wait after breakfast, you can use making decisions; thinking or writing down the goals of the day or just simply listening to a good podcast; listening to some cool music which helps boost your morning mood; or just make love if you have a partner; or do whatever makes you feel human, i.e. don't use it to check social media or the news. Use it for real; send that email you have to send, or just go for a walk. Also meditation can be good if you didn't do it beforehand. I usually like to meditate before breakfast, but when I do it afterwards, it feels great too. Actually, meditation is good at any time (as I am going to explain in the chapter related to meditation). So then, just do something with your life while you wait to go to the gym.

Once you are at the gym, and if you have no idea about what to do, you should pay for a personal trainer who can teach you, and make sure you start your gym life on point. It should help you because you are paying for it and you don't want to waste your money. It will also make you notice how much you can push yourself in terms of resistance or weights. It can also help you to understand how the gym works, where the things are located, how to use the machines, and it would make you feel more comfortable, like less oh-fuck-people-are-looking-at-me-and-I-have-no-idea-what-to-do feelings. I know that feeling of knowing nothing. Well, with a personal trainer you don't have to know much. After you finish your workout and go home, write down all of the routines this dude, or girl, just taught you in order for you to do it by yourself. But please be focused and enjoy it. Do your best.

Wear some nice clothes. Buy clothes that make you look cool. It helps with your goal. Going to the gym must not be to show yourself off to others, but for sure it would help. It is better to dress well than to dress badly. And if you have no idea about what to wear or what suits you, just go to any sports store with some good discounts and buy at least three different t-shirts and at least two pairs of gym shorts, i.e. six beautiful combinations. Then you can exchange them no doubt. Nobody really cares, it is just to be well-dressed and feel good about it; easy confidence points. You will see the difference between going with your very comfortable, but shitty clothes, and going to the gym with some clean and fashionable clothes. Of course, get some good shoes and some socks too; the complete outfit. You can't use a nice t-shirt with some shitty or very out of the mood socks. Be careful you make an analysis on yourself. Just ask somebody that is going to be honest with you about how well you look. I usually like to choose black, or white, or dark blue. Those colors are good for making you look serious, calm and focused. The very colorful clothes are for girls and people who go to the gym only to show off and stay on the phone 90% of the time.

When going to the gym, always have some water with you. Because you don't want to have your phone with you, so you will want something to replace it. My trick here is to use my bottle of water as my phone in the sense that I touch it, and I drink from it, instead of using my phone. I am talking about the bad habit of checking the phone constantly. It is also a good moment to check the view. Some good-looking girl or maybe some random-dude-good-exercise you can try someday. Just be in the gym mood. You have to enjoy it. When you go alone and want to have some music to boost the power, use it. Just don't be focused on it. If I am listening to music, I just turn the phone into flight mode. The more focused on the gym I can be, the better. I don't want to chat in the middle of my gym routine. It is a break from life. Relax.

About the workout: do a routine which you feel you are pushing yourself, don't do something easy. I like to warm up a bit before, and to do a bit of cardio afterwards. Run for never less than 15 minutes, otherwise it is like doing nothing. Don't do too much cardio if you are looking to grow some muscle, then cardio is not your friend. You should start with high reps of low weighs until you go for fewer reps of higher weighs. That is the gym philosophy for me. Also, while resting from one exercise, do another one that doesn't involve the muscle you just worked on.

One other thing, don't look at the other dudes with huge muscles. They have spent some years at the gym, so don't envy them. You will always find, as Michael Caine used to say, someone bigger than you. But you might also find someone who is in a less fortunate position than you, so don't compare yourself so much and do your exercise. When you feel like doing nothing, like you feel it is not your day, just go to the gym and do a light workout. Never try to skip one workout because you don't feel in the mood. Do it, it will make you feel better, I bet on it. Continue with the workout routine, and try to exercise every part of your body every week. If for life circumstances you only can go one or two days a week, do a full body workout. Full body workout means that you train everything: biceps, triceps, back, chest, legs and everything else. If I only go twice a week, I definitely do the full body workout, always starting with the back. The back and shoulders are the parts of your body that form the "v" form which is very attractive to girls. Try to focus on that. Focus more on the back than on the six pack.

Also, if you in fact have time to go to the gym more than twice a week, do leg day. Leg day is the most difficult day in the gym. But it is the one that gives you the most powerful boost afterwards. It helps you in all of the ways you cannot even imagine. Having good legs is equally attractive for men as for women. So focus on that, at least one day per week. Leg day also allows you to be close to the beautiful girls who are doing leg day. You can just ask, if you feel the connection, for them to teach you a random leg workout that you don't know. Also, one way to check if your leg day was right: just try to get down some stairs. If you lose balance or if it hurts a lot, it was a good leg day. Otherwise, you did nothing.

The core exercises that give me the most pleasure in terms of feeling great while doing them and after doing them are: shoulder press, bench press and pull ups. These three are without doubt my favorite ones. Therefore, I spend some time on them and I have been getting stronger. But you can have your favorite ones too. For example, another core exercise is the deadlift and all of its variations. But I really don't enjoy it; I only do it when I have to, when I am doing leg or back day. What I want to try to show here is that you can have any favorite exercise and become an expert in it. You will feel good and look good to others when you do it. Therefore, you will have some nice confidence. But always remember that it does not come for free and that it takes time and effort to master an exercise. Also, be careful, and if you think you are doing an exercise wrong just ask someone you think might know how to do it, or just ask to check if you are doing it right. This is the importance of the personal trainer. If you focus on learning the basics with a professional dude, it will save you some injuries.

If you are a master already in the gym you will probably understand all of the things that I am saying here. And you probably have your own routine which has been working for you for a long time. That is just awesome, just keep enjoying it. Just try new exercises, new workouts, like handstands and exercises related to improving your spine and the health of your bones. Just be open to trying new things. Gymnastics might be a good option too if you feel you are losing flexibility because of the weights. There is always an option and it is very dope you already have a level which you enjoy. For the ones who already have the gains with you and can see how all of the time has been worth it: just enjoy that feeling and keep on going.

As I mentioned before, it is extremely important to eat before going to the gym. But it is also equally important to eat afterwards. You want those gains to help you build muscle. So then try to eat a lot of whatever you want to eat. Just of course try to make it healthy. Some protein and carbohydrates are very good. I suggest not killing any animals to keep you in shape but everyone can decide. I said quite the opposite when talking about the breakfast with the bacon part, but the point is not to eat animals all the time. Truth is that there are some very good vegan options like beans with rice for example. This is a very powerful food. But of course there are multiple recipes on the internet you can cook by yourself or there are also many places in your city that you can go to.

Here in Sweden, I sometimes go for a kebab or a pizza, because it is not expensive and those are some gains. But again here, don't over think about what to eat. Just don't stress about not knowing what to eat. Don't make a big deal out of it. Be practical and save some money of course. But if you find something you want to eat, just do it. If you have no idea, pick whatever food you see first and eat it. Don't be very strict with yourself. One of the things that helps me here is to cook food for several days, then I know that once I get home I have the food ready and I can eat as much as I want. Cooking at home, with good ingredients, will always be better than eating out. I'm not saying this, it is Anthony Bourdain's principle.

You need to choose a good gym. Don't go to a depressing gym. Go to the new one or the trendy one. Do a survey with your people and try to find out which one is the one with the highest probability of finding the hottest girls (for inspiration), has decent machines and has the cheapest price. Do it. Also take into account that it has to be convenient but you can make an effort without any problem if it is a bit far away. Enjoy the freedom of going to the gym. And just do it for your mind and body.

When at the gym, make friends. You can talk to girls or boys. It is good to feel confident at the gym. Also, in the summer months try to do some outdoor workouts. Lately, I have been following this guy, Ido Portal. He posts some dope workouts on Instagram and YouTube. Yes, I know Instagram is crap, but like I told you, use it for good, not for bad vibes. Make your time valuable. Free workouts are welcome.

The gym is a routine for life. I have gained my body now. I went through a phase of putting a lot of effort into my body; now I am just chilling. I do workouts without feeling stressed about the outcome. I do the ones I like. I am not lazy. I still go when I feel like not going. However, I already have a big body so it is just about maintaining it. I do not want to get bigger. Now, I really want to get those abs. But it is fine if I do not get them. The gym is amazing. The more effort, the better outcome you get. Do it. Actually, if I could, I would only date girls that go to the gym. They do the best positions. They can do reverse cowboy with their feet on the ground and do those squats with high frequency and power (just like the doctor told you!).

5. YOUNG AND HUMAN

I was in platonic love with this beautiful German girl. She has had a boyfriend for more than seven years and I, by no means, intend to destroy her relationship. However, because of her experience and commitment, she taught me some valuable lessons. In the middle of work-related conversations, we talked a lot about love and life. Not too long ago, I sent her this message and she reacted with a heart, probably because I paid attention to her words:

"Every person has different paths to follow and the rule of life is that there are no rules, love included! I connected what you said, with what another friend said, and it's very basic: do whatever makes you feel right, that is the winner's life framework"

One thing you must know if you want to enjoy your life, is that there are a lot of ways to live a life. Most of the media, the movies, the books, the YouTube channels and the people in general talk about how you should live your life. Then, when you compare your life to what they say, you see that it doesn't seem that joyful or great. Every time you didn't have a girlfriend, you wanted one, and now that you have one you want the freedom to go and flirt with other girls, or just be with your friends. Or in any other situation, people are taking action on your behalf. Then you start hibernating, you start doing things you don't even know why you are doing them, because it just seems right. I don't think that is a great way to live life.

The great way of enjoying life is to accept that life won't ever be perfect. Life will always find its way to complicate things and to push us to act like human beings. We are humans after all. We are people that have the capacity of having an infinite number of different emotions. We can be sad, happy or frustrated, or whatever, but this is it, this is life. Life is to enjoy all of the feelings and to be thankful for having the chance to experience them all. If you were not alive you would not be sad. What I want to say is that there is no problem with being sad. You can't be happy all the time. This is a very big lie. You can be sad sometimes, it is not a problem. You can be angry, you can feel hungry, you can be satisfied, you can feel anything. The capability to appreciate the bad and the good moments in life is the key to living a meaningful life.

Furthermore, what we should not do is to feel nothing; to be cold, to be stone-faced and doing things without any purpose. Going into automatic pilot mode is terrible. You need to feel alive, you need to feel something. The bad things will be over sometime and the good things too. Neither the bad nor the good last forever. Enjoy the beauty of the music; the beauty of a girl in the street; tasty food; all of the small things that come into your head. Just be alive enough to appreciate this. Don't get caught up on what you should do in order to be happy. That is not the main goal. The main goal is to live a life that allows you to walk down the street, while breathing the fresh air and looking at people you don't know, smiling for reasons you have no idea but you can playfully imagine. Destroy your ego to be able to know more people and establish more human connections. Demolishing your ego would take a heavy weight off your shoulders, and will allow you to go throughout the years lighter, more authentic and more human.

Keeping in line with this argument of living life as it is, bear in mind that you have to be patient. In the movies, the dude who finds the love of his life only takes one hour to find her and it is quite easy and natural. But life is not a movie. Life will probably last for more than 80 years, so that means each day doesn't have to be lived as if it was the last one. It just needs to feel right. To feel that at least you did something with your day. You accomplished some of the goals you set in the morning, or the day before. Life will surprise you and will show you some opportunities, but you need to be ready for it. As

Picasso used to say, "Inspiration must find you working". Good things come not by magic, but by hard work. Don't think a miracle is going to happen. There are no miracles in life; it is just luck and hard work. Yes, and hard work with some direction, because it is the same as doing no work if you are working hard on something that will take you nowhere.

For example, the gym would make you look better for sure. If you keep smoking cigarettes, that might take you somewhere else in your life. So be bold and choose what you spend time on and work for. Life is full of things to do; don't be complaining too much about having nothing to do. If you have found no passion yet it is because you haven't tried that many things yet. Get out of the house and do something. But of course, here is a very important point to highlight: everyday life is not the day your life changes. There are some days that change your life for good or for not that good, but not all days have to be the most awesome days. Normal people live normal lives and that is completely ok. It is completely fine to have a normal day in your life if you are smart enough to appreciate it. Focus on feeling alive, as I said before.

If someone in the street doesn't say hello to you; if someone looks at you with a bad face; or if someone does something that makes you feel uncomfortable, don't let that ruin your mood or your day. Just focus on not depending on people to make you feel alright because they are as human as you are. They probably have dilemmas in their lives and put on masks to overcome those scary feelings inside of them. And those masks can be good people acting like bad people, or bad people acting like good people. You will never know until you know the people deeper. So just don't let your mood be strongly correlated to the attitude of others to you. You are you and you should take care of you. You do what you can do, and about what you can't do, just don't get mad if it didn't happen.

One thing I want to mention on this topic is the ability to not ask for favors. The less favors you ask for, the more people like you. Nobody likes to lend money or to do stuff for someone else in general. People just do it when they are in a good mood, and some people are, but others are not. The less you ask from people to give you stuff, the better. So that dude that is almost your friend but not a close one yet, don't ask him to cut your hair for free. I did it and it felt awkward to be honest (Laughing emoji). What would you give him in return?

The world is not served for you. The world is the world and you are you. You have to give something in order to get something. That is how it works. Also, don't give too much expecting too much, because people also have the tendency to get addicted to receiving without giving. So just be equilibrated. Keep your life together so you don't rely too much on people to solve your problems. First of all, always try to solve your problems yourself. Then if you can't, you can look for help, but otherwise don't make yourself feel bad asking for favors. The less you can bother people, the better (I say it here again). Of course don't get me wrong, just be smart enough to understand the situation that is happening. Unify not bothering people and giving first instead of receiving first and you will have a more compact life.

Don't get addicted to watching videos on YouTube on how to pick up girls and how to transform your life. You get some dopamine from that and what will happen is that you will eventually not do what the videos say you should do, but instead, you will feel pleasure imagining your life in those situations from the comfort of your room. Your room must be a place you enjoy. If you don't like where you spend half of your life, then half of your life will not be that nice. If you have a bed that you enjoy, it is a huge step towards satisfaction with life. So make sure you enjoy your bed and your pillows. Save some of the money that you are not spending on parties, alcohol or drugs, and buy a good pillow. Use nice blankets.

Check out the light in your room. I personally like the "yellow weak" illumination which causes the effect as if I was using candles for example. A candle you can turn on to illuminate your room is also a nice thing to have, for you or for the person you are going to spend the night with. A good rug that is in balance with the colours of your room will help you to keep it cleaner. I recommend a rug because I use it as a shield against dirty shoes. I don't come inside my room with dirty shoes because I don't want to ruin the rug. Therefore, I avoid having dirty and smelly shoes in my room. Swedish people are good at this: shoes are forbidden inside apartments. They have these nice racks they put their shoes on next to the front door. This is a good technique.

Make sure the walls of your room project your age and maturity. Don't stick up a poster of a half-naked woman as if you were 12 years old. Keep it nice for yourself. Remember that if you invite a girl over, she will analyze you by the way your room looks like. It requires effort, time and money to have a room you feel comfortable with, but it is worth it. When you have those feelings of not going out because the party is too far, or because you just don't want to go out that Friday night, you will always have this nice bed and blankets waiting for you. It is a nice feeling. You need to appreciate it. For me, when I don't go out and I have tea instead of a low alcohol beer, I feel grateful for having the opportunity to sleep in my bed, and then I don't feel like I am missing out on too much of the fun.

About the FOMO, fear of missing out. I can say it should be balanced. You can have it because it is normal, but you have to understand that one in ten parties would be fun. One in ten parties you would say were totally worth it. The other nine, if you are single and in the constant search of a girl, you would feel like you went out for nothing. That is how it is. If you have a higher ratio that is awesome. But as you grow older and become more mature, you learn to better select the nights you want to go out or don't. It doesn't mean that you stop going out, or that you stop taking the chance to go out for a night that apparently doesn't look good. You just learn to increase this ratio of good nights.

You are not forced to go out every Friday and Saturday. You can stay at home and cook. You can work on a Friday night. You can do something for yourself. Again here, please bear in mind that all I want to say is that it is OK not to go out the night that everybody else went out and you didn't feel like it. It is ok to feel like that. We are not full of energy and full of motivation all the time. Life is tough (and majestic). You have to put on your best mood and face the challenge. But you can also just chill and don't blame yourself for it. Life is short but actually is not that short. Taking better decisions would be much appreciated by your physical and mental health.

6. MEDITATION PAYS OFF

This is a very special part of the book. Meditation has been one of the most wonderful things I have discovered in life. It came to me after I had a few panic attacks and I didn't know what they were at the time. One was before getting on a flight in Amsterdam, and the other one was just on a normal Wednesday night in Bogotá after a football match. The trigger for these panic attacks was the stress and anxiety of waiting too much for this world to give me (success in all aspects), without me putting any effort in to getting it. Or actually, feeling that even though I wanted to put effort in, I just could not deal with the fact that I was in a broke-trap. I was definitely forcing my mind and body to do many things in a short amount of time and all of them involved concentration. I thought that keeping my mind busy was enough to keep bad thoughts away.

But keeping yourself busy is not the right approach to not having bad thoughts, as you might be thinking. You should not depend on external facts to keep you calm or happy. And of course, this is something you just learn with pain and suffering. You need to be aware that peacefulness is not in the soccer game, in the night out with your friends or in your work. Peacefulness and mindfulness, which are strongly related to a happy life, are inside you. You don't need to look for solutions outside of your life. They have to be the complement to your life. But your inner self is you and nothing else. Therefore, you need to train yourself to be able to cope with the positive and negative situations that life will put on the menu. And here is where the concept of meditation comes in.

I have done meditation on a daily basis. I have skipped some days of course, but I have been engaged with the practice for more than three years, and it has been extremely important to opening my eyes and seeing the world with a strong mindset. In the beginning, you just need to learn how to breathe and how to focus on the breaths. There are techniques for that. In meditation you have to count to ten and then start again with your breaths. If you lose count because a thought appears, you should just acknowledge it and come back to your counting.

You learn to pay attention to the things we don't ever appreciate with this breathing technique. We do body scans that allow us to feel every part of the body, from the head to the toes. We feel the sensation of being in a seat, so you feel every part of your body that is making contact with all of the surfaces that are holding it. We also feel the sounds we didn't even realize were there, for example, the tick-tock of the clock, the distant songs of the birds, the neighbor's music, or simply the sound of the air passing through your body and feeding your soul. Those are methods that keep you concentrating for several minutes on a special task; just checking out what is going on with your body and your mind.

Apart from the basics, there is meditation for everything. You can find meditation for anxiety, pain, heartbreak, fear, motivation, thankfulness... and so on. There are some very cool apps I strongly recommend. The Waking Up App by Sam Harris, Headspace and Insight Timer are my favorite ones. All three are freemium and offer an interesting variety of different meditations that only do good for your mind and body. If you have noise cancelling headphones, or even with the normal ones, put a Spotify playlist on from the Meditation genre, lie down, close your eyes and breathe. Breathe deep and fast, and exhale slowly. Complement it with a sleep mask if you want a full sensation. Falling asleep is allowed.

Meditation is as equally important as exercising your body with yoga and gym. Meditation is the time of the day when you connect with yourself and get some knowledge of what is worrying you at the time. Having the ability to check your worries from a far away distance, and not getting inside them is one of the most beautiful and amazing aspects of meditation. It allows you to see all of the priceless things you have in life. Oprah Winfrey used to say: "Check out what you don't have and you will never end the list, but check out at what you have and you will find more than you thought you had". And I relate this beautiful quote to meditation, because when you meditate you see what is really important and what you should be worried about and what not.

Also, if you need to be worried about something, it will give you the training to overcome it in the best possible way. When we put life in perspective, everything can be bigger or smaller. Therefore when we learn how to operate our mind, and we stop being ruled by our minds, life changes. It changes, not because you are taking control of your life, but because you are stopping trying to take control over things you cannot control. You just let it be. You are building a resistance against every obstacle that can come into your life. Mindfulness doesn't end the fear of talking to a girl; the fear of losing your loved ones; the fear of missing your friends; the feeling of loneliness; the feeling of low self confidence and everything you can think about. But it certainly teaches you how to manage that emotion to use it to your advantage, and to feel it without judging yourself for feeling it.

To learn how to do it properly, check out the apps or ask a friend that knows how to do it right. My words here are just to motivate you to take action for your mind. There is no need to make a big deal from a small problem. All problems seem small when you put them in perspective. I got very angry because my router broke and my corridor mate did not share his WiFi password with me. Like honestly, what kind of square young dude does not share his WiFi password with his corridor mate? It is just as stupid as me getting angry about it. It feels bad, but man, it is such a small problem or anger. Putting it into perspective, I ended up just smiling about how insignificant our problems can get.

There is no need to feel you are awkward and lonely in the world. That feeling does not last forever and the truth is: sometimes we are awkward and lonely. We are humans. You are not the only one with problems. The empathy with other people's problems that meditation brings, can lead you to live a better life in the way that you, and one million other people might be feeling the same, at the same time. We are living souls and we do love other people. We want everybody to feel good about their life, so everybody wants the same for you. Don't fool yourself with the news. I will talk about that in the next chapter. But for now, just go out and try to count how many good acts you can see on the streets; a small act, like a person saying thank you in a natural way, to another one. Do it, we are all together. We can all be happy and free.

Square and thin skin people are out there too, just relax. They are inside their boxes. It is not them, but their narrow-minded souls and egos speaking for them. Be chill about it. I have this friend that plays football. He is a beast. When he plays he always goes hard. I have another friend that is also a beast. We played together yesterday. They constantly crashed against each other until one of them stopped and was like: what the hell! While kicking the air with anger. The other mate, smart as Stephen Hawking, said: "El que se enoja pierde Samuel!" (in English would be like: "the one who loses his mind, or lets anger dominate the mind, is the one that loses"). Such a great mantra to live life by.

The last important aspect I want to mention in meditation is the capacity to be thankful. Yes, no matter what, you should be thankful for the good and the bad that happens in your life. It is something again that you might learn in life the hard way, but it is better to put it in your mindset now to prevent you from becoming crazy when the tough times come. Be prepared; be ready to face heartbreaking situations. You will cry. Be ready to be kicked by life. And of course be ready to let life surprise you with the infinite positive and amazing things it has to offer. If you want to learn how to be thankful, you should learn how to meditate. With meditation you will realize all of the things you have that you didn't even notice before. The list of things to be thankful for would be infinite. You can write down every week, (I don't like to do it every day), five things you are thankful for. It is pure mind medicine. You will see in the long run how amazing this is for keeping yourself together and strong under any circumstances.

Of course, we always want more, we always want better. We always think that what we have, or we are, is not enough. It is ok to feel like that. We are in a constant search for satisfaction. It is alright to aim for better always, but we have to appreciate "the now" too, because the present is all we've got. We keep looking for something. People, in a lazy and small effort, call it happiness. Other people, like Jacob, a close friend, call it 'what makes you enthusiastic'. Others say it is the reward of the people we are looking for. So, for any of the purposes you have in life, you will feel you are getting there, you are making progress and you are experiencing it, when you stop for one minute to be thankful.

An easy and simple technique when you wake up feeling down, or you are feeling down at any moment of the day, is to take a sheet of paper and a pen. Write down three things you are thankful for: a small one, like being able to have a glass of water, a medium-sized one, like, being able to work on your project today, and a big one, like being able to call that person you love with all your heart at any moment of the day and just hear his or her voice (Cheers to Gustav for that tip). Practice it, master it and enjoy it hermano.

Meditating all day will probably not bring you any money or any good news. Don't overdo it. Meditation is something that should be done in the right amount, to create the basis of your life. Your life is meditation if you want to become a meditation teacher and make money out of it. But if you want to feel good, and you want to better understand what meditation is for, you have to go outside and face life. You have to keep trying things. You have to get out of your room. You have to write the book you want to write; you have to pass the exam you need to pass; and you have to fill that long job application form.

You will not find happiness in meditation; it is not designed for that. Meditation itself is not happiness. Having a meaningful life might be, I don't know, it depends what your motivation is. But don't expect that because you are meditating, everything in the world will be better. No, that is not the point. The point of meditation is to prepare your mind to face all the challenges that life brings. That is it. It is one amazing tool you carry on yourself to go out into the concrete jungle and follow your heart and dreams. Also, do not forget that dreams without any action remain dreams. Do not be a dreamer, be a doer.

Meditation is like the gym. It takes time to see the benefits. I have done it for over three years and now I do not need to do it every day. I can do it whenever and wherever. It takes literally almost no time to do. Only ten minutes a day, or even five, and you will get it. I do breathing exercises every day though, but not the full ten minute meditation. That one I do like three times a week. The less you meditate, the more anxious you are. To achieve this level (confidence in practicing it), I did meditation almost every day for over two years. That is how I learned the technique: pure hard work.

Currently, I am loving the cold showers because they make me present in the moment. Being hit by the cold water in the morning, to the rhythm of your favorite music beat, is priceless. But also, if during the day I am losing control of my stress, I take long, deep breaths and exhale super slowly. It is the fastest way to calm myself.

You can try it right now. Breathe deep and exhale slowly.

It is so worth it to master meditation. You can get High on your own supply like Wim Hoff says. I am still learning more meditation techniques. I am getting new coaches and exploring different methods to keep it fun. You do get bored of doing the same one every day. A journey of exploring different techniques is always highly recommended. To finish this chapter, I encourage you to smile more in life. We all know what it is like to be sad or to be happy. We get in our heads so much, we start doubting what other people will think if I do this, if I do that. But no one cares. Life rewards people who are willing to break free from their own insecurities. If you think people actually care, then know that people respect adventurous men. Dare to take risks. Enjoy the adrenaline of taking action, the rush of aliveness.

As a side note to this chapter, improving one's life takes courage. The best way to not be worried about life is to take decisions and actions. Jordan Peterson has tremendous good content about it. He states that you need to have a vision of your life: what type of friends would you like to have? What type of family? What type of partner? What type of job? The answers will keep changing along the way. But is it important to pick a way, and work towards it. Including meditation in your daily routine will allow you to check the progress of that vision. Meditation itself is an effort.

There is no life without effort. The interpretation of your life must come from you, you have to create it. No one else knows your life better than you. No one else can go to the gym or meditate for you. Being a nihilist, in the sense that it's worth accepting that life is meaningless, is the easy path. Easy paths lead to self-destruction in the long term. Now that you are in your 20s, or whatever age you are, is the moment to know yourself better. You have to do an evaluation to know at what time you would like to wake up every day and to sleep every day. Your mood depends on how much you are able to stick to a routine. No routine, no productivity, no hard worker feeling. Motivation comes from working hard; it comes during or after the work, rarely before it.

7. HEALTHIER HABITS

I want us to have good mornings and good nights, forever. You have to maintain a circadian rhythm to be fit for life. Do research about sleep quality and how it affects everything (I am no sleep expert). I just know that we should wake up and go to bed at the same time every day, otherwise, we will feel tired, experience nightmares, or get insomnia. In this chapter I only talk about having a good morning routine and a good night routine, but there are an infinite number of good ones. Those that are easy to judge as beneficial and adequate, those are the good ones. Have common sense when choosing them and you will develop, with commitment, some virtuous ones.

My friends Andre and Gustav launched a podcast called Habithon, which is about good habits. They are starting out, so their content is pretty unbiased and honest. A parenthesis here; always try to support people in the wellness industry. They are doing good for humanity. I am going to start a business related to wellness too. I love the topic, and you work, you get better, and you meet fit and healthy-minded people. I am starting to educate myself more on the business side, and then I will go beast mode into the project.

Coming back to the healthy habits, my take on the topic is as with anything in life, you have to try until you find the routines that make you a better person and make you better too. There are some horrendous habits, like not brushing your teeth after lunch for example. We are not going to talk about them because they are easily spotted, and there are so many bad ones that I am not even going to guess the most popular ones. Instead, I am sharing here morning and night routines to kind of set the structure for the day. The morning one, I briefly mentioned before, but now here you have it in more detail. All of them are a compounded investment. Besides, having a morning routine is equally important to having a calendar with your daily and weekly tasks. When you work this will happen automatically for you.

You will literally start your day by checking what you have on your calendar. When you study it is the same; you check on the calendar which classes you have. In life, your calendar is among your good friends. If you do not do everything that you are supposed to do, if you do at least one of the tasks that was on your calendar, that is still better than nothing. Ideally you will do everything, starting by waking up with a morning routine, and by the end of the day, you will be proud of yourself; no regrets on your mind because you did what you had to do. But it's fine if you do not do everything. Life is all about perspective. I promise, if you stick to a morning routine, a calendar and a night routine, in the future (give it three months), you will stop one day and say: this is normal for me, while other people would say: "oh man... you are god".

Healthier Morning

I support the idea that the first few minutes of your day are going to define your mood for the day. If you wake up in the right mood, nothing can stop you from feeling good. Therefore it is very important to create healthy habits before going to sleep and after waking up. If you wake up feeling down, or angry, or worried, let it go man. Get up and do not let destiny decide your life. Create your own.

You can sleep as much as your body is asking for, but, it is not very productive. You will wake up around 11:00 AM and you will probably wonder whether you should have breakfast or lunch. Not good (to start the day having doubts). On the contrary, if you wake up at 9:00 AM then you will know that you have to cook some breakfast because there is still time for lunch to come. First thing: wake up as early as you feel comfortable. If you can start your day at 6:00 AM, do it. But if you are waking up early and then feeling tired all day there is no need to do it. A good night's sleep is fundamental to keeping your mood and energy levels up. So, try to wake up between 6:00 AM and 9:00 AM. If you are working or studying, and you have to push your waking up time earlier, then do it. Nothing is mandatory here; you do what you feel better with. However, stick to a routine. It means, you should try to go to sleep every day at the same time and wake up more and less at the same time. You will see how well you can feel when your body has an organized schedule. Not everyone is a morning person. So relax when other people tell you to your face, that they wake up at 5:00 AM, go to the gym, read a book, bang and take a shower by 6:30 AM.

After opening your eyes, the first step is to check the phone to turn off the alarm (or buy a $5 alarm clock, as Simon Sinek says). Do not stay on the phone checking messages or social media, or news for more than five minutes. Just turn your alarm off and that's it. Do not start your day wasting any time. Nevertheless, do what you want to as long as you are not getting the feeling that what you are doing is not right. Then, after turning the alarm off, the next step is to drink a nice big glass of water. There is no better way to start the day than with a glass of water, and maybe a multivitamin pill. It feels incredible. Then, you can just enjoy going to the toilet if you need to. Put a nice smile on your face because you are alive for one more day. Life gives you the chance to be alive for another day and that is something you have to be thankful for. So, drink that water.

After the water I usually take my towel and go to the kitchen. I start by mixing eggs, usually three or four, depending on how hungry I am. You can put whatever you want on an omelet. According to one of the people I consider a beast in many ways, Anthony Bourdain, cooking an omelet is mandatory for every human being and the way you make it says much about you. I usually put cheese and bacon. Other days, I only put spinach if I want to feel I am making a healthy breakfast. Other days, I just put in some salt and pepper. I just try to change it up so I do not get tired of eggs. I just put the eggs in the pan on a medium-low heat and go for a shower. I know in fact that my shower will last for at least two songs that are around three minutes each.

So in six minutes, after I have finished my shower, I come back to flip the eggs and let them cook on the other side. You should know this is a trick I stopped doing, because I moved to another place where it is more complicated to shower and cook the eggs at the same time. But you will find your own way to do it efficiently and fun too. Now what I do in my new place, I shower first, then go to the kitchen with my kindle and read and cook, no music, just cooking and reading like a beast. Recently, I moved from omelets, to scrambled eggs. You change; your eggs too.

But continuing with the story, once I leave the eggs cooking, I prepare my music. I pick two splendid songs to put my mood on the level. It can be any song with a happy beat (like Veronica Maggio's Jag kommer). It means that the notes do not go lower but the opposite happens. When you listen to the songs you pick, you have to feel the up beat. It can be rap, electronic, house, techno, or jazz. Just try to choose a happy sound. You will realize if you are listening to a sad beat or a happy beat. If you have a sad song that can also give you the energy and the vibes to start the day with the best attitude, just do it (like Veronica Maggio's Tillfälligheter). Put it on. Vary them. I am always discovering new music. I use Spotify radio for the songs I like, and it works pretty well.

With those two songs I take the speaker, or phone to the shower. I put them on, then I start with warm water; the first ten seconds, warm water. Then as the beat starts to get nicer and nicer, higher and higher, happier and happier, I start putting the water colder and colder. By the time the chorus of the first song hits, the water is very cold, almost freezing. This is very good for the body. First, it wakes you up, even if you do not want to. Second, it puts you in the right mood because you were not afraid of starting the day with cold water. Third, after you finish your shower you will not feel cold when you are not under the water anymore because you are already cold and fresh. Fourth, apparently taking cold showers improves your immune system. You can check it for yourself. I stopped getting sore throats and colds after only showering with cold water. And fifth, you just feel very fresh and clean. I have to repeat it: I strongly recommend cold showers

Then I just go to the kitchen, flip the eggs, put the bread in the toaster and go to my room. I get dressed and play a podcast. It can be about any topic you are interested in, but lately as I am interested in the Energy Transition, I am just listening to podcasts related to this topic. You can choose from a variety of apps. It will make you feel smarter while you put your clothes on and while you have your breakfast. It is good to learn something new every day. For me, the podcasts in the morning are the best way to do it. Business people like Donald Trump (I am not a supporter, but I have read his books to understand his mindset and also, the guy is president of the United States), argue that for business it is better to be a generalist than to be a specialist. It is better not to know less about more and more, than more about less and less. Podcasts, when you listen to them, can pass you knowledge. Nothing like books though. If you can read a book instead, do that.

I still support people who want a calm morning without any noisy distractions. Not even a podcast, or a good song. Having some music detox is also good, and I do it often. I take around one week without listening to my favorite music, or sometimes, no music at all. Then the moment I listen to those beats again, it feels so freaking good. You have to balance everything in life. Too much music or too many podcasts involves too much dopamine. They will get you less and less excited. Be careful with that. Not only with music, but with food, and any other pleasure you are giving yourself too often.

Then, after you're dressed, just jump into the kitchen and serve your eggs and toast. It is a must to eat fruit too. It can be a banana, it can be an apple, just whatever you like. Just try to change it often. Not a banana every day and not every day whatever. In variety is the pleasure. Also, I usually cut lemons and make some lemonade. Yes, just lemons and water, nothing else. It is very good for the immune system and also feels extremely refreshing. You can have some juice of whatever you want, just try to pick something fresh. Do not buy ready-made juices. Those are too sugary, they taste very weird and are very unhealthy. The less chemicals in your food, the better. Always go for the fresh stuff. Yogurt is good too. It is a superfood. It gives you all the good bacteria your body needs. If you check the internet, you will find the dope mental wellness benefits it brings too.

While eating you can choose if you want to enjoy your food or enjoy your phone. Of course, the choice is the food. Put your phone away. You can keep listening to the podcast, but do not be on your phone checking messages and that stuff. Eat in peace. Focus on one thing. Enjoy the feeling of starting a new day. Beautiful things will happen. You are putting the energy you need on yourself. You will be fine after having a good breakfast. Taste the food; I know it is hard, but stop and taste the food. I make the mistake very often of eating too fast. Then, whenever I remember that there is no point in eating fast and not enjoying the food, I eat slower and I can taste more of it. The more you chew your food, the easier for your body to process it. You feel good before, during and after eating. If you eat good food, it will happen. Food is medicine.

After eating, I meditate. Meditation is the most important trick to keep my mind working during the day. Nothing really stresses me out after meditating. You can't control the thoughts your mind is creating, but you can take a step back and notice them. You can just notice them and come back to what you are doing. Meditate. It takes ten minutes of your day, but it gives you a very rewarding feeling of being mentally healthy. Do it after breakfast when you are preparing yourself for the day. Yes, it is worth putting your alarm ten minutes earlier just to have ten minutes to meditate. You will notice the difference. You will feel calmer, more present, more chill, like, more human too.

Then, here you are, ready to start your day. Of course, do your hair, brush your teeth, shave, put on some aftershave and do all of the stuff to keep your appearance clean and healthy. Enjoy your day. In this part, you can replace your food or exchange the steps or just take out some or add some others. Breakfast is never mandatory; when reading Tim Ferris you see the pattern that most successful people like Bill Gates skip it. Fasting has benefits for sure, but for me it is about trying out new morning routines and sticking to what works. We change and our morning routines will change too. It is a mix between taking out of the routine what is not working, while exploring new ways of making it feel better. For example, doing a 10 minute workout every now and then after waking up, and sipping the cold water next to your bed is not bad at all. It will put your blood circulation on point, and wake you up. Gustav from Habithon does this in the mornings. Do it, try it. They have a free course on that. The essentials, for me, of this part are: cold showers, breakfast and meditation, and no phone, always no phone. Only for the alarm, the music and the podcast, not for news or social media. Stick to the morning routine.

Healthier Nights

To get home tired is one of the best tips to keep in mind to having a good night's sleep. Therefore, to be tired you have to do things during the day, you have to move your ass. Get out of bed and do something for your life. Work or study; do sports and read.

Something that allows you to burn calories and exercise your mind and your body. I prefer to be outside of home. So try to do all of this outside your house, room or apartment. If you like to work or whatever at home you can definitely do that, but I do not recommend it. Get a co-working space, or work from university. The productivity gains of having an office are unbelievable. Once you touch home, it will not be working time anymore. Respect the spaces.

It is good to meet people, to see people, to look at people and to say hi to people. It is also nice to have the feeling that you are doing something you feel proud of. So, if you are working for your company, if you are writing that book, if you are doing something productive, you will have the feeling in your gut that you are doing the right thing. I recommend working with things you can tell anybody and feel proud about. When doing something during the day, imagine yourself for a moment talking about what you are doing on the national radio for thousands of people (like my finance teacher Julio Villarreal used to tell us). Would you still do it? Would you do it better? Would you keep going? That is what motivation and purpose is. Enjoy that energy boost. If this is checked, then we can start with the routine you can try to follow, or modify accordingly to your preferences. This routine is for the normal days, the days nothing else is going on. You are not having this huge party or this fancy dinner. You are not seeing that friend, or you do not need to study all night. It is for the normal nights, for the normal days. For life is also normal. Not every day will be crazy-crazy.

Let's imagine you arrive home after your working day is finished. It is whatever time you usually arrive home, but we can say that it is between 5:00 PM and 8:00 PM.

Go to your room and take off the clothes you were wearing outside. Do not bring your dirty shoes into your room. The shoes that have been outside must be next to the door of your room or next to the entrance of your apartment. Do not allow dirty shoes inside. Follow the Nordic tradition, it is nice. When you take off your shoes you will feel how your feet immediately get more relaxed.   Get dressed in some comfy clothes, the clothes you wear when you are at home, the comfy pajamas. That is something fun. Usually the clothes we wear to look good are not that comfortable, so then here we are saying to ourselves: well done, but now let's try to get into the night mood.

I guess you might be hungry. So if you have not cooked any dinner yet, prepare yourself something that doesn't take more than 30 minutes to make. This is common knowledge, but I mention it because we need execution. We need to move from knowing stuff to doing stuff. If you check a recipe, ask for a recipe or know about a recipe, make it. Do not wait ages to make it. Do it. You can check out some recipes on the internet that tell you how much time it takes to cook, and will also tell you exactly what ingredients to buy. Those recipes are usually found on supermarket websites, or just use Google.

Recently, a friend of mine recommended checking out a recipe online for chili con carne and it was absolutely amazing. It took me less than 30 minutes and it was very delicious. Go for something you can cook quite fast, that is tasty, but that is also friendly to your digestion. Try to not eat much at night. It is not that healthy. Just cook some of these quick recipes with some music. Again, if you want to listen to another podcast, do it. If you want to check some random YouTube video you can also do it. If you want to check your phone, do it. No social media of course. If you want to read an interesting article, do it. Just do whatever you want to do while waiting for your food to be ready. Here, try to pick recipes that do not involve too much cutting of onions and that stuff, that takes more time, but it is up to you (I accept I am not the fastest at cutting vegetables).

Remember, keep it healthy, tasty and cheap. Actually, do not get me wrong here. First, if you like to cook for the whole week and just heat dinner up, that is dope. Also, it is worth spending money on good ingredients and getting your cooking skills to the next level. I am just talking about the days when you are tired and want to chill. Some days you feel like cooking good stuff. That is good. With company, two times better. Healthy, comfortable and fun. Maybe, if you live with someone, or many other people like me, match your schedule with them. You know why? Families that eat together are less likely to have their children become drug addicts or get into illegal stuff. If you are used to eating together with people, you are less likely to create negative and self-destructive thoughts. So as long as you can, do not eat in your room, eat with your roommates. It is good to have good relationships with the people you live with, even though you can hate them on the inside. Just joking! It is a waste of time to hate someone.

So, by this time it might already be 9:00 PM or so. Check your phone one more time. Do it, no problem. Do what you have to do. Do not drink too much water before you go to bed. It is so much stress to get up and go to the toilet. So, keep your water consumption kind of low after 9:00 PM. At night, eat light. Your sleep and your dreams will be finer. I suggest that after, or better during dinner, you make yourself a nice cup of tea, some tea that makes you sleepy and calm. Those teas you find in every supermarket and the brand I don't think it really matters. Just pick one that says "good dreams", "perfect nights" or whatever related to it. If you hate washing the dishes, do not worry, everybody does, even the ones that have a machine for that. However, I suggest cleaning everything as soon as you are finished. Also, dry the dishes and put them away. You will thank the future you in the morning, after waking up to a lovely clean kitchen. Do stuff. That is what a grown up does. You should keep your place organized. Of course your room too. But here we are just talking about the kitchen. So, we end this scene with you in your pajamas, with a cup of tea, heading to your room.

This is very important (do not get nervous). Here comes when everything can go bad or can go well. If you keep being on your phone, you can end up checking the time and realizing that you have been doing nothing for an hour (I know you can relate). So, try to not touch your phone. Instead, have a book you enjoy reading. Get a Kindle, it is cheaper than to keep buying physical books. When buying a book, buy a book you really want to read. It can be about any topic, really, about anything you might be interested in. I do not recommend these famous classic books, like Marcel Proust or James Joyce, because they are hard to read and you can get bored easily. So what I recommend here is to go for something more practical.

You can read for example about leadership skills. You can read this book. Yes, this book is perfect to read at night before sleeping. So, if you are doing it right now, I wish you a good night. But, yes, back to the point. I was saying that instead of touching your phone, go for a book. If you really do not like reading, you can go for any streaming site like Netflix or HBO (or audiobooks, even better). It is alright. There is no problem with it. Do not blame yourself for being addicted to one series, just do not exceed your limits and try to sleep after five episodes. If you watch too much of a series you will get tired of it soon, even if it is the best series in the world. Try to go episode by episode. If you want to know how it ends just then go to the last episode and watch it from the last five minutes. That is not the right way to watch a series. You have to enjoy and appreciate every episode. So if you are reading, you might notice you want to close your eyes after half an hour or so, and, if you are watching a series, you might feel your eyes heavy after an episode, or two. Of course, some episodes last longer than others, but let's say an average duration of 40 minutes per episode.

Again remember, you are in your room with the light on or off. I prefer like in the middle, like the light from a candle; darker rather than brighter. So, enjoy your book or your streaming. After you finish, just take the decision to close the book or to turn off the laptop/TV/phone. You should block the blue light from your devices when you are having dinner. There are some apps that allow you to do it. Blue light is bad for your sleep and your sight. There are many apps. I recommend one called "Blue Light Filter Night mode" for Android users. Try to do the same for your TV and your laptop. iPhone has it on its iOS, and so do other devices. Put this filter for like two hours before you plan to go to bed. Also, when you wake up in the morning you will not receive that strong light from your phone that hurts. Instead in the morning you will see a nice dark screen. So, after you set your alarm, send the last text, check the last thing you wanted to check, put yourself in the sleep mood.

The sleep mood is to lie down with the lights off. If you need to go to the toilet once more, do it. No problem. I remember I was scared that I was always going to the toilet to take a piss before going to bed. I talked to the urologist and he says it is the most normal thing in the world. If you are younger than 50 years old, chances are, and very high, that your dick is healthy, so relax. That means nothing, just go. Afterwards, lay in your bed. I suggest lying on your back, face up. Then think about all the things you did during the day, from the moment you started it. Just a quick review of what you did. Do not judge it; you are just having a picture of what you did. Then, just take some deep breaths, close your eyes and let your mind follow your breath. Try looking with your eyes closed. Try not to think that you have to fall asleep now. You will fall asleep eventually. Do not force it. Your body knows how to fall asleep. Let your body rest. Breathe and exhale slowly; keep calm. Any thought that appears in your mind, you can just notice it. If it is something you have to do tomorrow just write it down on a piece of paper, or put it in your calendar on your phone.

You can just adjust your last step before sleeping as you want. You just need to have this routine and follow it. Try to follow it every day of your life. Again, the circumstances might be different as time passes, but the essence might be the same. If you are having trouble sleeping, count. Yes, count like in the movies. Try to count backwards, that is even better. Count from 1345 to zero. Eventually you will get bored and will feel like changing the position of your body and you will feel this sleepy beautiful feeling. Remember, from your bed you will not solve any problems, so, it is not the moment to worry. It is the moment to relax and sleep. If you need a solution, the solution to the problem you have on your mind will very likely only come when you are not looking for it. So relax, keep calm, be patient.

Do not move. Enjoy lying down. You can remember positive things that have happened in your life. You can even think about three things you are thankful for. You can also keep your eyes open and let them close naturally with time. Just relax. Smile. Yes, you can have a smile on your face. The fact that you are smiling will somehow help you to smile for real. Close your eyes, enjoy your sheets, smile and breathe. Sleep will come, for sure it will come. Relax. Enjoy. Tomorrow will be another day. It will be another day to live.

You spend about a third of your life on a mattress. Do not be scared of investing in a good one; the ones that are from brands with above average prices, known for providing the most suitable ones for a good rest. If you sleep well, you already win the next day. Give it the importance it deserves. Respect your sleep times. My latest acquisition was a $30 sleep mask. It completely blocks the light and is very comfy. It is even 3D. You can open your eyes, while the mask is on.

I wish I could be like my dad. He goes to bed around 8:00 PM every day, and the moment his head touches the pillow, he closes his eyes, he listens to the radio and he falls asleep. He is a sleep king. He has mastered the art of sleep all his life. Even when life got tough, he still managed to sleep well. Problems never stop coming.

So it is good to let our bodies know that the bed is to rest, not to worry. Other things also matter like room temperature, quality of the air, quality of the sheets and position of the bed. Take action now. You do not want, believe me, to reach your sixties with sleep problems. You do not want to reach your sixties regretting not having taken action, or risks in life. You are young now, exploit it. It is the moment to use your body and your talents. What you do is what will define you. It sounds too common to say, but it is the truth. Action is king, the king of kings. You have literally nothing to lose, you either win or learn. And you will sleep better, because you will not think about what you could have done, because you actually did it.

8. QUITTING NEWS GETS YOUR MORE TIME

News is just so much misinformation. They literally control what people talk about. I do not see the Yemen war, or Libyan slave trade as often as the dark humorous talks of Trump. Or, the very VERY small problems of the northern developed part of the world. Just honestly, quit quick news and social media news.

I have become more productive since I quit checking the news as often as I used to check my social media. Usually, the news is talking about a multinational company that is going into bankruptcy; a terrorist attack that killed people in some part of the world; the decision of a politician to do something stupid in public; the words a famous person said during a press conference; the uncomfortable situation in which a famous person was photographed; that climate change is happening faster than it was thought; China along with the US and Europe in a dispute over trade and privacy laws; Africa's struggle with their dictatorships and progress; corruption cases emerging every now and then in Latin America; the release of a new music album by a pop star; a video of a normal person that went viral on YouTube; the results of your favorite football team; a new medicine that could cure cancer; a new virus that might be the most dangerous one ever created; and so on.

So you get the picture. Multiple news stories about multiple topics that literally will not help your life for the better. They will not make you more productive. It is not something that would touch you 99% of the time. It is like when I was a kid in high school and I was not able to take my cell phone with me. I used to say I had the phone with me in case something happened. They said, the school board, if something happens they could call your parents without any problem. So it is the same. If it is news that might affect you positively or the opposite, the information will get to you. So yes, basically, checking the news is something as addictive as social media and takes as much of your time.

You are consuming information without any context and this means you are learning nothing. You could never understand the conflict in the Middle East by reading a 200 word news story. If you want to know what is going on in the world for real, go for magazines that publish articles that are at least ten pages long. In those articles you will find information that is relevant to understanding the context of the news. News is just fast little lies (half truths). It is an instant addiction. It is something you look to see if something terrible happened in the world. It is literally like a casino, because you never know what you will find. You will check that news website or app all the time to see something; it can be shitty news or good news. You do not really care. You think you care but not really. It is something that only feeds your desire to consume news. It goes nowhere.

Based on this, I recommend that you go for magazines that focus on certain topics and that you can learn something useful for your life or for your conversations with others. It is not the same to say that Donald Trump is a bad president, as to say the reasons why Donald Trump has been a bad president (with strong arguments and facts). You will become a wiser person this way. Instead of reading ten news stories without any context, pick one topic you are curious about and read a full story on it (do not be the annoying person that brags about how much you know with people you do not know).

I have many options for you, but you can look for the magazines that charge you even just a couple of dollars but will provide you with some, of course biased depending on the belief of the magazine, but more contextualized information. As one of my teachers used to say, if you put the neoclassical glasses on you will see the world this way; if you put the conservative party glasses on you will see politics in another way. So in order to be able to create a solid argument, a nonbiased one, to understand the truth: take care and consider the source you are reading from.

I am not saying you should not be aware of what is going on. It is just to stop being addicted and losing time doing it. Instead you could have organized your room or done some work. Always remember that the less you use the screen, the better it is for your mental health, for your happiness and motivation. Sad news can make us sad. Happy news of course has the opposite effect. But sadly, newspapers know they might get more readers publishing more sad news. Therefore, they can play with your brain and make you think that the world is marred when it is not.

Search on Google why today is a better day to be alive. Then, you will find uplifting information about poverty, CO2 emissions, access to water, wildlife population and all of those topics that every newspaper is not talking about. Yes, it means you should look for happy news. It is better, like listening to happy music instead of sad music. If you listen to sad music you will get sad. Then, of course, you want to be sad sometimes and that is ok. But with the news, you get sad because a couple of words are telling you that the world is on fire, because a terrible news story just appeared on your screen. Then you will be thinking that the world is evil and humans are the ones to blame for every bad thing.

Humans are the best and most intelligent species in the world. We are good people. We are! You have to understand that. Not every day and not every minute, but in general we are good people. What we have achieved as a society has to make us proud of being on this planet at this time. Past times were not better than today. New medicines, new foods, new clothing, new planes, new cars and the views of the world have been evolving through time, to make our life easier and more comfortable. Of course, everyone has to make a profit and you have to work your ass off if you want to achieve something, but that is how the world works. It is not bad or good. It is just how it is.

So, try to reduce short news consumption and instead go for full articles. Remember, the world is fine, do not think it is a place where everything is bad. No, it is not. The world is fine. Keep that in mind. Also, if you do not like something, you can do something about it or you can do nothing. It can be a small step. For example, you can choose what is going to be your fight and your objective to help the world with something. Mine is climate change. Climate change is my fight and I want to work to move towards renewable energies in every country of the world. I would love to fight for it and see the results in fifty years. But other things, like female genital mutilation, which is something I find terrible and sad, is not my fight. Helping people with not enough food to eat is not my fight. It is something that if I can help, I will do. And I am of course willing to help whenever I can, but it is just not my fight.

You have to choose what you want to fight for in order to improve the world, one step at a time, and then you become good at it. Pick one; you can't pick every problem that is appearing on the news every day. Pick one, stick to it and improve the world. You will not improve the world by reading news. That is just not going to happen. If you are not sensitive anymore, whenever you read something sad, do not say that the world is a mess because you are not even feeling anything. You have the right to complain about whatever you want to complain about, but if you complain about something and you are doing something, it feels more right in your life. So, small actions, less talk, more action. Less meaningless reading, and more sweat.

Do not think you know everything because you have been checking the news every day all your life. You might know nothing. You might think you understand something but you don't. Be humble with the knowledge. And if you do not want any biased information just read about the same topic in different journals. You will see the difference.

You will see that what they write and the way they write it can change what really happened in real life. So, be careful. Enjoy the art of accepting that you know less than you thought. If you want to know about the war in the Middle East, read a full research paper about the topic. I had no idea that apparently it was the US who funded the Iraqi army to fight Russia in Afghanistan. Iraq won the war but also got so many arms that they took the opportunity to go against the US. Arab people are very likely to get into wars because of their long history and unforgiven battles. Do you think I learned this in the daily newspaper?

News and social media. Big waste of time. That is why, sometimes, life feels fast, hopeless and lonely. Now memes about news are also going crazy. Black Lives Matter movement, COVID-19 theories and a bunch of publications that you are forced to read and believe. Politicians fighting against each other is always big in the news, then people pick a side and fight too. The politicians, because they are sneaks, they keep doing their politics business. The people end up being divided, and poorer. This is just so stupid. The news wants you to get involved with emotions on this stuff. But it is better to get involved with facts and research. Be educated. Do not waste time with uneducated people.

Not too many people have the right to give opinions. If you are going to give one, do your research before. You know the people that talk crap all the time. They exist, they are all out there. Do not be one of them. Stop sharing fake news. Your life will get happier by choosing, not finding, but choosing, a purpose. You say I want to support the world with this, and then you do something. Focus. News is addictive. It does not make you smarter. Smart people read 30-page articles, or books about topics. Be that person, and not the lazy one reading 100 words, thinking he or she is an expert. I finish with this: just relax, spread peace and love. The world is good. We are evolving and getting better. Do not get distracted!

9. FOOD AND COMMON SENSE ARE MORE EFFECTIVE THAN MEDICINE

We only have one body and one mind (some ungrounded people still think they can damage their body because they have a healthy one underneath). We can't take for granted that we are going to be healthy all the time. We have to make it happen. The highest probability of dying young is related to car accidents or fights. So, do not drive drunk, and do not drive under the influence of any drugs that can change your reality. Also, avoid being in a car with someone who is driving under the influence. In addition, do not get involved in any bird-brained fights while being drunk. Do not get in a fight because you wanted to fight that night or at that moment in your life. It is not smart to get into fights in the street. It is very lame-brained, especially if you just found a nice girl, and if she is educated enough, she will not like that. If by any chance you see yourself in the middle of a fight, just run as far as you can. If one of your friends is trying to start a fight, be his friend and do not let him fight.

If someone is going to steal your phone on the street, let the thief take whatever he wants. Material things can always be replaced, but any undesired circumstances might end in a very bad way. Also, do not do pinheaded jumps or very stupid actions you know might get you really badly hurt. Also, do not do it under the effect of any drugs. I know this is something you might already have on your mind, but it is good to read it, and for me to write it. It is something that should be in the basics of keeping you healthy. We can all have fun and enjoy life without putting it at risk. You will probably remember this short paragraph when you are in any of these kinds of situations. Last but not least, use a helmet if you are riding a bike, and use protective equipment when you are doing any kind of sports.

These are just the basics to not getting physically hurt. Sometimes we forget all of them. But remember, everything is alright until it goes on the fritz. You were super safe in your neighborhood walking around at night for eight years, until one night something unexpected happened. So take care of the future, create it and prevent yourself from getting any bad news related to your body. On the other hand, if shit happens, which can happen, that is life and we must deal with it as the men we are (you can feel sorry, and cry, but still you have to deal with the problems). Dealing with those kinds of setbacks requires compromise and self love. We have the ability to recover mentally and physically from any bad situation. It is just a matter of time.

Besides these basic ideas to increase your probability of living longer, you need to take care of yourself when having sex. Again, you never got any STDs or you never got anybody pregnant until it happens. So do not wait for it to happen to take the decision to use a condom. To use a condom is to show yourself some self-respect and self-love. It is also a good way to demonstrate to your partner that you can be very horny, but your mind is always in the right place.

You really do not want to be the dad of an unexpected son or daughter. I do not think it is a smart idea if you are still learning how to take care of yourself. Eventually it would be nice to have children, and to share a family if you want to. But when young, dumb and broke, it would definitely make your life tougher. You will have to face the challenge it brings. You will have to deal with real life and you will do the best job you can. I do not doubt it. But it is better to have the things in life at the right time and when they are really wanted. Or if you already feel ready for it, go for it. But use a condom if it is not in your plans. Just do it. It is cooler to use one, than not to use one.

If you get laid with the same girl multiple times, then discuss it and talk the talk. When was the last time she got tested? And, is she using any kind of contraceptive? Share your answers too. If it is a girl you are only going to have sex with for one night, do not even ask (you should actually but we know sometimes it probably gets a bit weird), just use the condom. It will not kill the vibe. It will make you feel better the day after. You are investing in your future happiness. The moment, the excitement and the craziness of the night will not disappear by using a condom. And as a grown-up reflection, it is perfectly normal to want to know your partner's sexual health regardless.

Another way of keeping yourself healthy is to have good eating habits. Basically, you should consume carbohydrates, fiber, protein, some fats and only water. Tea is good for you. Juices and soft drinks are bad for you. They are. The less you consume them the better. If you feel like having a Coca Cola someday, just buy it and drink it (maybe not all of it). But do not do it all the time. This is just basic with everything related to food. Do not eat so much of something. Do not eat burgers or a lot of burgers very often. Do not eat spinach every day of your life. There are more than 20,000 different vegetables starting from the letter "A" for artichoke and ending with zucchini.

In the intermixture, in the balance of having different kinds of foods in your stomach, you will keep yourself energized to live. Excess is the cause of many of the diseases when you are 65 years old. So, do yourself a favor and create the habit of eating healthily. It is something you can do, and enjoy. I am not telling you to become a vegetarian if you do not want to, but decrease your meat consumption as much as you can. If after watching very dramatic documentaries (Cowspiracy, What the health? to mention just two) you still want to keep eating meat, do it. Just be ethical enough to know where the meat you are eating is coming from. Meat involves the death of an animal.

Chickens are the ones that live in the worst conditions you can imagine. So at least, buy some EKO eggs. When you boil eggs from hens which have been in cages, versus hens that have been walking free, the color of the egg yolk is so much better in the ones from the free-range hens. Most people forget this, so I am going to say it. Eggs are chickens, animals, they have moms. Be aware of what is happening in the world which lets you have a nice piece of beef served on your plate. This is just culture. It is called education. If by knowing all of the facts you still want to do it, do it. But remember, eating red meat is extremely unhealthy for you and extremely bad for the planet (colon cancer according to a Harvard publication, and a lot of methane, insane water consumption and deforestation where it is produced).

I heard the other day that changing from red meat to chicken causes the same impact on the planet as if you change from chicken to vegetarian. It kind of makes sense. Small efforts produce small benefits. It applies to everything in life. So I am not telling you to be drastic about your food choices. When you think about it, it is a bit messed up to eat meat. It is. So that burger that is super tasty is a dead animal. Deal with it. If you like it so much, reduce the number of burgers you have a month. Give a chance one day to a veggie burger. Be open-minded about food. There are millions of recipes and tastes that are waiting to be discovered.

Do not let yourself be controlled by the media. Have an honest opinion and make decisions after knowing the facts. For me, watching all of these documentaries opened my eyes to the point I became vegetarian. For almost one year I tried hard. Now, I just do it as much as I can. Life is not black and white. Do not put labels on your actions. Live the moment. Enjoy the food. If you eat a burger every Sunday night, you will not appreciate the amazing taste of the burger, the same as if you eat the same burger once a month. Take better decisions when it comes to food. Eat a lot of vegetables. Eat a lot of fruit. Try to change the menu. Do not stick to the same food you love. Keep trying new things. If you find a new food you love, then repeat it. But do not over eat it. Be calm. Also, it is cheaper to cook if you are vegetarian. Meat is quite expensive.

And do not forget that fish also suffer when killed. Plants do not get sad when the seeds are taken away from them; they do not suffer pain and they do not know if they want to die or not. Animals do not want to suffer pain. Be conscious, if you do not want to change completely, decrease your consumption. Be the one showing how to rock it to the new generations. We must be accountable for the planet we are creating for our future children, grandchildren and infinite-ish-grandchildren.

If the social pressure is too high for you, eat with your friends what your friends eat. But show them that you have a point. They can create a collective interest in eating healthier and it can become a cool thing to do. I try to go at least once a week to the veggie restaurant in Lund (they offer more food than other daily lunch places too). If your friends never want to try veggie, I doubt it, but in case it happens, you should get some friends with healthy food habits. There are no secrets and no hidden information about the benefits of having good friends. Be selective. It is true. You become what your friends are. And you will eat what your friends eat. So, again, think about it. Make decisions.

I am not saying stop being friends with someone because of the way they eat. Again, it is not black and white. But if you know a friend who knows a really tasty vegetarian place, you can go there together. Also, if she/he knows a veggie recipe. This is it, be smart. Love yourself. Same with partners, coworkers and family. Family is a bit harder, I know. But would you not like your parents to drink less soda, less coffee, eat less meat and be healthier? It is our responsibility, as global and educated people, to pass the message to our parents. If we give a damn about it, they will listen, and will give a damn too.

However, do not over think when eating. You might feel very bad if you are unhappy about not eating what you want. Choose what you want. If what you want is not good for you but is tasty, eat it anyway. Make yourself happy. It is OK. You deserve it. Do not go for excess again. When I was suffering from gastritis, I changed my diet drastically for about one and a half years. Then, the stress of choosing what to eat and what not to eat was also affecting me. The solution was to eat everything but on a wiser way.

If I feel like having a juicy burger, I will have it. But until I really want it, I won't have it. Sometimes, the desire of having that juicy burger is just a momentary thought. With meditation you might be able to learn to differentiate the feelings of your body from your thoughts. You might think you want it but again it might just be a thought. You know how it feels. You are human too. You know the feeling of drinking water when being thirsty. So, if when feeling very hungry, you think about a burger and this makes you feel this amazing true feeling, do it. Make yourself feel happy. Do not care about everything else in that moment; you want your burger, you go for it. Do not feel bad about it. It is human evolution and economic development giving you the chance to eat that tasty burger.

Drive yourself with good emotions. After you finish it, do not feel bad. You did what you had to do. You are full now, and it is time to move on with your life. There is no necessity to think about the past. Do not lose time on that. You will do better in the future. Do not forget at this point that, if you stop for example, smoking, you will eventually not feel the need to smoke anymore. With meat, in fact, I know it's kind of the same feeling. If you stop eating meat, you really will stop the desire to eat it. This takes time but it will happen.

Sugar is like that too; with coffee too; with salty food. The less you do it, the less you miss it. It is possible to change your diet, and not suffer a lot when doing it. It takes time. Be patient. Yet, if you want to eat that cake, eat it. Just do not eat cake every day. If you go to your grandmother's house for dinner and you are a vegetarian, chill. Do not say no to food that is cooked with love (even if what grandma, friends or whoever cooks, sucks). This is called healthy food habits: you are living your life while you are also getting pleasure from food (among other sources).

Furthermore, be aware of the quantity of energy used to produce your food. The transportation, the land used, the storage and then the transportation to the supermarket. All of these are the benefits of being alive in 2020. And it will get better every day. Like two hundred years ago, people did not even have the chance to eat beef when they wanted. You have the chance to eat a burger if you want to, thanks to capitalism, economic development and technology. You do not need to eat it every day. But knowing that you can do it at any moment you feel like doing it, from my point of view, is something relevant. It is something you must appreciate. You must be aware of the millions of opportunities of different recipes you can get nowadays. Go and explore.

Enjoy the economic development. If you are a burger dude, I insist because I am one, enjoy it. But keep trying new foods. Give new restaurants a chance. Support people that are chefs. After reading Medium Raw: A Bloody Valentine to the World of Food and the People Who Cook from Anthony B., I have much respect for the cooks. Read books about food and watch recipes from the famous chefs that are available. It is food porn; it is literally in a bad way, food porn. But who gives a damn? It's nice to try to be a chef. You could always order a pizza if you screw it up.

Be aware that it is so much cheaper and so much healthier to eat at home. Home cooking wins over outside dining, always. Read all of Anthony Bourdain's books or any other rock star chef (do not read the boring ones). Get inspired about cooking. Learn how to cook; how to make pasta. Do not put ketchup on pasta; there are a million sauces to put on pasta. Respect the classic recipes! Eat salmon. I usually do the lemon juice in the mornings and to be honest, almost any meal I can. I drink a lot of tea, but without caffeine. I take care of myself. I do not mind spending more money to get better food. It is your health; food is medicine.

It matters so much to give the body the right fuel. Always buy vegetables and protein. Never forget about the nuts. Almonds, I saw on the BBC, are the most powerful food. Do not forget sweet potatoes. Every blue zone in the world, wherever there are many people living longer than average, eats sweet potatoes. They plant their own food and engage a lot in the community. Balance it up. Lately, I have been eating a lot of salads and sushi. These trendy salad restaurants are a good way to go: they make it very green, yummy, and healthy and prices are fine. We must support more people that are opening healthy restaurants than the typical "new burger" ones. And even as a burger fan that I am, I do not remember when the last time was that I ate one.

I am also doing poke bowls that cost around $13 bucks (including misu soup). Japanese cuisine is fancy and healthy. It is my favorite. I still need to learn how to cook those recipes though. Their chili mayo, uff! It is also dope to go to Japanese restaurants with girls. The lighting is usually good, and if you are eating aphrodisiac food, you are on the way to enjoying your sex more later. There are a ton of options; be healthy with food. Love yourself. Love food too though. It is a bit dickish, to say eat good bla bla bla. Well, that I know costs money.

Not eating cheap bread every night of your life is expensive. Work for it. Work your ass off to eat good food. Escape the poor trap of eating low quality meals and then getting sick in the medium- to long-term. I don't eat candies at all. I pay a visit to my dentist every six months for cleaning, and everything is fine. In general in life, using common sense, the expenditure should always be more on healthy stuff than unhealthy. Work hard, eat well, but not too big portions. In Sardinia, the Italian island, people live longer because they live surrounded by friends and family but also because they are always eating under their calorie needs. Treat yourself, bon appétit!

10. BUSINESS, EDUCATION AND WOMEN

These three words are connected. The more educated you get, the more likely you are to get into business, either earning a high salary or starting your own company. It feels great to build your way up to the top. Education and wealth is a big recipe for getting better at networking. When you master the art of networking, more people will know about you. These people will either have a good image of you or a bad one. You cannot control the fact that you will not get along with everyone. It takes time, years, to build your social network. Your image must be one of a charismatic guy, hard worker, creative and fun. If people know you for that, girls will start to notice it. Whenever you go to a social event, if they know who you are from before and they have a good picture of you, you are already winning. Having a good picture means that you broke free from the trap of not being able to be who you are. You are not scared to talk about the topics you find interesting, to raise your voice when you want to give an opinion on others people's topics, and just to develop the mindset that Mark Manson promotes of not giving a fuck.

However, there are many rich and educated people that are not confident. They just do not know how to get a network, without paying for it. If they ever get one, it is because they were interested more in the money than in everything else. I guess you do not want a relationship with your network that is based on your money or your social status. We all want people to like us because of who we really are. Dare to be authentic all the time. Every life is different. You, the way you are, your body and your mind, is unbelievably amazing but it is not enough. No one gets confidence and awesome stuff by just existing. Confidence only comes when you deserve it. If you have nothing to feel confident about, how are you supposed to feel it? Faking it gets you nowhere in the long run because you know you are not what you are projecting. When you have truly worked on yourself, you know what your worth is (same when you know you have been doing nothing).

If you want to be good in business and with relationships, in simple steps it will be like: go to university, get cool friends, get rich, and be cool. It is not an easy thing at all; they all take time and effort. If you invest in the things you find interesting, you will reach master level in them. And as Derek says, there is no need to reinvent the wheel. If you have someone that has already accomplished what you want to achieve, pay for his or her advice. We get into our own beliefs and we think we know, but very likely we don't. I see it as when going to the gym, you think you know, until you get a personal trainer. The difference in the training and the results are clearly visible. Getting a mentor is a great investment; for education, for friends, for self-development, for everything. In Sweden, I have met people that turned into my friends and made me better. I did not pay for them; it was my energy that attracted them. On the other hand, I remunerate people when I want to get shit done. Having someone that can keep you accountable is worth it. I just got one to create sales funnels for Software as a Service companies. We are all different; no one can give you the fish, but me, or others, can only teach you how to fish. Go for what you believe in.

When you feel certain about your self-improvement, you project that image. At the moment, the girls I get in my life, I don't even know how I get them. It just happens. I am not desperate and I am not projecting my insecurities because I am working hard on them and I feel proud of my work. It is not that I need to brag, or feel superior, but I don't owe anybody anything (besides my mom, my dad and my brother). I am me and my contribution to the world. Sometimes I said pretty dumb things, and maybe I was not even looking the best (this might actually not be true). However, my attitude, and my mood of the night were on point. Or, if I knew them from before, my attitude towards life was on point most of the times we interacted in the past, and they know and feel it. It is a very popular idea nowadays but it is true: what matters is not what you say, but how you say it. Also, what matters is who is hanging out with you. Are your friends a disaster, or are they cool? What type of parties are you getting yourself into? People do not fit in every type of social gathering.

It is alright if you want to sleep with many girls. Girls that come to Sweden want to ride Swedish boys too. It is like that, everybody just wants to get laid here and anywhere in the world. If they are single, they will probably want it more than if they are in a relationship. But everyone is thinking and talking secretly about it. Do not even think about feeling ashamed of wanting to sleep with Swedish girls (as many as possible, as beautiful as possible, and bla bla, or you want to find "the one"). Girls are also human beings. You go out and you see the scene of the guy and the girl leaving the party at 1:30 AM, and in your mind, you know what is gonna happen. You ask yourself, how did he do it? Other girls will be like, why is nobody going home with me? It works differently from men to women, but everyone wants to get laid. They screen men and if they don't see the value in you, nothing is going to happen.

Men get hornier easier; women need more work. Read about human nature. I remember watching Jay Alvarez, a lady killer, saying that we are all just dots in the world. Girls and boys, we are all the same, but different. The difference is probably in our body, but we all want kind of the same things. You have to treat women as human beings, not as princesses. Some girls like to be treated like that, but you will not sleep with them. For someone to be with someone, it has to be at least at the same level or at a better level in life than them. No one that is a ten will sleep with a five, if they have the chance to sleep with a ten. Be honest with girls, as Mark Manson says. Just be you. Be honest if you only want a one night stand or a relationship. Be honest about what you are saying. Forget scripts, and all that pick-up bullshit. You just gotta be you. But that "you" must have accomplished something for humanity. There are many people that exist in the world, but why would someone go home with you, or on a date? Are you a valuable person, or are you just existing? If you fake it, would you like to be with someone that has fallen in love with a fake you? Are you going to wait until you turn 45 to realize that you contributed nothing to the human race? Working on a meaningless 9 to 5 job will not be the smartest decision.

You better stop thinking that girls are hoes for not sleeping with you, or because they are sleeping with many guys. In Sweden, a girl can sleep with 100 men. No one judges her. No one. Why would you? Who are you to judge a girl? (You may be the guy that jerks off to a ton of ethically disgusting porn videos). If a man fucked 100 women, then that would be alright? No, it is the same. Sex is mainstream in 2020. If you judge, you are in 1950s. In Sweden, girls have a lot of sex with whatever partner they choose. Sex is nothing crazy. Some people may like it that way, and some others may find it too liberal. Well, everyone can choose what they like, and what they don't like. I personally do not care much about it. You should not judge the past of a person; it is toxic and it will not only bring nightmares at night, but also at breakfast time too.

In Sweden women have rights. They are empowered. They know more than you. Nordic countries are better when it comes to quality of life because they have more women taking decisions (a huge number of CEOs and in politics). They are educated and they have money. All the patriarchal tricks that people use in other countries will, in most cases, not work in Sweden. You will not buy them with a drink. They will pay for their drinks and their dinner. Here is another top point. Here you get better quality women. You get the good ones; the ones that like you for who you are. Of course, in other parts of the world you can get them too. But here it is more likely. More quantity and more quality. To get girls you need to be a gentleman. This strategy never gets old. Like, a confident-nice gentleman. Never a macho attitude, because here they are independent women. Like, confident-nice-funny ish. Never like overprotective, or over-provider. Cool yes, and good looking yes. When in the encounter, be like playing a tennis match with friends, when you play to win you lose. When you play not to lose, you win.

Integrity plays a big role in the Nordic life. You cannot be an angel in the street, and a rat in the house (sorry for the bad word). Men and women behave in any situation, in any place, at any moment. That is how it works. Integrity is about self-respect, self-love, and about respecting others, and loving others. You would never do something you will be ashamed of. You would not do something that will harm someone else's feelings or body. You would never take advantage of someone because she knows less, or she is passed out drunk. We must respect each other. We must take care of other human beings. No, never ever can someone sleep with someone without consent. It cannot happen.

Common sense when dealing with a critical situation will be the guide. If you think what you are doing does not look good, do not do it. No one wants to feel used. It does sound awful to talk about this, but it is important. I feel like when someone invites some friends for dinner, and then the host says: please do not use the tablecloth as a tissue for your nose. I should not be talking about this in this book. But there are these people out there that are completely stupid and animals. No offense to animals, but animals do not think about the consequences as we should do. In Sweden, most people respect each other. It is not a kind of utopia, but it is a well-educated society. We must promote respect in the world. Integrity is more than not using and abusing people. Integrity is about also having standards. If you know you will not enjoy sleeping with a girl, do not do it. The goal is not to sleep with many girls, but to have fun, enjoy the experience, and meet new people. Have limits on what you allow to happen in your life. Say no when it is required. If it is not a big YES, then probably it is better not to do it. The law, life and the people will demand punishment for those who cross the line.

Do not be desperate about girls. Get a life man. Get friends. Enjoy hanging out with the boys. If you have a life, they will come. To have a life you need to make decisions. If you need to quit your job, quit friends or even talk less to your family, for your sake, you do it. If we want to get better in life, we need to cut what is holding us from growing. That involves hard decisions. I miss my parents but if I hadn't moved out, I would have been way less experienced and mature. We need to grow up. Life is marvelous when you make progress. Cut the past and open the future. The boys that are your brothers will be there for you always. But, you will meet new great and inspiring companions as you get out of your comfort zone.

Getting girls is even a bit dumb to mention in this book. I didn't even want to talk about it. They are not these perfect creatures that are unreachable. They are not gods. They are as real and insecure as we are. I am talking about them just to express that the direction your life needs is not towards getting more girls. If you work hard on yourself, you will get them for sure. If you do nothing, you get nothing. Good quality girls of course. Like the ones that have less self-love than everyone else, they are easy. But maybe you do not want to have that. I want someone who is smart, beautiful and fun. The person and the relationship have to be fun. Fun is so important for me lately. If she is pretty, but not fun, big turn off. Girls will come. Relax. Do not think about them all the time. They will feel you are impatient and uncomfortable. When you stop using Tinder, looking at hot chicks on Instagram, and just stop getting bombarded with this fast and easy sexual culture, you can focus on yourself.

Be addicted to something else, like in Trainspotting 2 when they talk about heroin. It is not easy, they, the companies and the hot unreachable girls, just want your money. There is no free lunch in the world economy. The harder you work (on every aspect of your life), the more control you will have over this stuff. When you do not get any girls and you get crazy, you are less likely to get the first one. You get one, boom, then all of them seem easier now. It is because you are calm; you are open, but calm. You have to find your own strategy. Be yourself. Talk however you talk, and talk about the topics you find interesting. If you are having fun, she will have fun. If you feel comfortable speaking, she will notice it. You want to lead the relationship. You want to at least start it on your own terms. There is no point in feeling bad about a toxic person. People rarely change. There are good ones out there though. You will get them for sure (if you go beast mode in improving yourself while enriching the planet).

A related topic to networking is education. For me, the more I read, the better I get at conversations. I read about many different topics, so then I always have something fun to talk about when meeting someone. If you are good at networking, you will likely be good at business (and with girls). To be good at business, you need to be careful with money. And, there must be a passion for work. Working on the weekends as usual, like Drake, checked. The more educated, the better. Finishing a degree must not stop you from keeping you educating your brain. We all need to be lifelong learners, academics for life. The older we get, the clearer we see what we would like to learn. When we finish high school, we have to choose something to study right? And, it is very likely that we just did not have a clue what we wanted to do in life. It was dumb to answer how you see your life in five years, or ten years. With what experience can you answer that question when you are seventeen years old?

Normal people do take the decision to study what they thought was right, and put effort into it. But after we get old, we know where the feel-good knowledge is at. First, you need to try and not give up. But then you can study anything. Mastering a skill that you love is priceless. Being smart and educated is attractive. So, find what you like, try out different stuff, like, for real, go fishing, go hiking, do coding, whatever, until you find the sweet spot. You will not be able to find your passion until you have been open to new adventures. Travelling can get you to new adventures. But it will never fill any voids in your soul. The motor of your life is your inner self and it can only be developed by acting.

If you are going to travel, do it with a purpose. Do not do it to find yourself. Do it to do good for the world. Pick a community you want to help; pick a world problem you want to fight with your hands; engage in sustainable programs; be a volunteer for teaching kids; work for free to companies abroad; do stuff, but do it in community. Traveling alone can be overrated. You get in your head too much if you do it wrong. The more you educate yourself, the more you can work on what you believe in and the more you can travel with a purpose. We must be responsible to do good for the world. Do not complain that the world is unfair, when you literally have not given anything to the world. Just existing is not enough.

When you get good results in life, you feel you know everything. Afterwards, the peak comes down, you start having this period when you get nothing, and you start questioning if you actually know something about anything. There are ups and downs that mean nothing. Do not get too sad if you are not getting results. Do not get picky, and brag too much when you get them. Be humble. Learn from mistakes, but be nice with yourself. Life is hard man. It definitely is. It is not comprehensible. No book can explain it. It has to be lived.

Life just needs a guy willing to take risks, and to have fun. To make sacrifices, work, study and go to the gym. Feeling low is normal. Especially when you thought you were going to get that job or education opportunity, but you didn't. It is alright. You keep trying. There are so many, but so many opportunities in this world, that you shouldn't feel bad for that one. Look for what fits you. If you do not like certain opportunities, why are you even applying for them?

People talk a lot about how to get girls. There is no recipe for that. Just exploit your talents. Be humble. Be funny. Everything that everybody usually says is true. But the connection man, the connection you only get with certain people is magic. That stuff is pure magic: being in the right place at the right time, looking in the eyes of that soul. Meeting the love of your life can come randomly, or you can also build this relationship. You see there are no formal structures, just attitudes. Either you want it or not. Dress well and don't get drunk. Chill. Relax. Nobody understands girls. Not even them (girls). So relax.

You do you, they will do them. Yes, they are also watching videos and reading books about how to get boys. It is the same. So life happens. I wish you the best of luck with them. We need more luck than anything else probably. You increase your luck if you do the right things in life. If you have already found the person you want to be in a relationship with, just enjoy. Make it better. Invest in it. That is another discussion. But, just enjoy it. It can end any moment. Literally, do not fuck it up. And, if the other person does, have self-respect, be willing to walk away. Focus on education and on the business. If the money is coming in, you are fine hermano. If you are learning, you are fine my brother. When this connection comes, uff, just enjoy it man.

Life is amazing. Stop thinking that until you get a girl you cannot travel, or live. You do not need a girl. You can do everything without a girl. The more complete you feel in your life without a girl, the more attractive you become. So please just chill. Enjoy life. Not everything can be fucking-fucking. Playing football, watching movies, reading books, going to the beach, etc. Do not stop living because you do not have someone. Live life improving yourself and this someone will appear along the way.

I have been asked many times: how do you start a company? I have no answer for that either. It only depends on the motivation behind the idea. You will find your own path. Get a coach; reach out to people, someone that can teach you the good practices of running a business in that sector. The calmer you are when making decisions (a product of being confident in the work you have done), the better they will be. Making money is tough. It requires long term vision. Learn how to communicate properly. I am learning as you can see. I have not mastered it. I am honest when I talk with people, customers or business partners. If I am smart and I am honest, that is someone the other person will trust. If they trust you, they will buy your product.

Sales is something you can learn. I read the Jordan Belfort book, The Straight Line Technique; it is a good read to master the art of selling. For product development, it is just a matter of trying a thousand times until you get the right one. I probably did 500 presentations of Xertify until I understood what was valuable for our customers, and how much money we could charge for that. Again man, no secret recipe. All these books can do is to tell you to get out of your comfort zone, make 500 calls, follow your dreams without being ashamed of that, and make it by magic. Do not waste your life being in your room. Get out! Not everyone wants to be a millionaire, and not everyone can be. It is not easy, it is not for everybody. Life is fair-ish in that sense.

One trick for business is to get involved in a community of entrepreneurs. Everyone will be creating companies, and for sure your imagination will multiply. You will likely get some knowledge spillovers that will make your life easier. Instead of paying $1000 for something, e.g. a logo design, a video, a talk with an important contact, you will know you can get it for free, and in two hours. People that have launched successful companies are authentic humans who understand other humans' needs. I have much respect. It is easier if you are rich, and you already have the network. In the U.S., if you have the right friends, and you pitch the idea properly (there are so many takes on this too, it depends on the industry, the city you are in, and the type of investors you are talking to), you can easily get a million bucks for your project.

People from less advantaged backgrounds have to work ten times harder. I am not saying the rich do not work hard. Those motherfuckers work even harder. I, again, have much respect and appreciation for them. They are beasts. They know money does not grow on trees. The best tip may be to love what you do. Or at least, to love the income you get from what you are doing. You have to work on something you believe in. That is when money starts coming in. No need to be an expert. Nobody knows anything at the beginning; it is just a matter of experience. Joining accelerators, incubators, getting friends that already have businesses, and getting educated are key too.

In Silicon Valley people are super kind; they will talk to you, listen to your idea, and even agree to meet in person. The moment you ask for something, you have to give something back. It is the rule of life. If you ask for a letter of recommendation, if you ask for a favor, think about what you can do in return for this person. That is how business relationships start. All the superficial and fake meetings and talks can in fact turn into money, pure cash in your pockets. It can happen, no secret formula, just winner mindsets. No room for cowards, or for shy people. It is like being in the jungle, a global jungle. Businesses are truly global (COVID-19 proved it). So you are competing with people from all over the world. That just makes it so much nicer.

More innovation, better companies. More competition is always healthy for the planet. Everyone has to work. The good ones will make it, for sure, no doubt. But it takes time. I would say at least six months to have a product, another six months to have product market fit, six more months to start doing some sales, and one more year to start accelerating the income. Easily more than 3 years before you start seeing the results of the hard work. It is like that. You take it or you leave it. You want to work your ass off for the next 20 years and live a great life afterwards, or you'd rather do it chill and mediocre for 50 years, and have an average life (average in the sense of having financial stress and emotional voids)?. More money, different problems.

Money buys happiness, better health, better friends, everything. Endless ambition is never good of course. It is not about being an obsessive money-making person. It is more about working for what you want. You will not have this energy forever. You better use it when you have it. That is all I am saying. You will not be young forever. Reach a point in your life in which to get money will not be a problem; to get girls and having cool friends is not a problem either. Why? I have money, I love a girl, or I am a happy single person, and I love my friends. I do not care if the lunch costs $20 today. I just want a life in which money does not stop me from doing things. Normal stuff, not like I cannot buy a yacht :(. No, I am talking about everyday living. Money is out there to live more comfortably; to be healthier in the mind, the heart and the body. But you cannot expect to receive it without giving something. There will be no free lunch in 2020, or in the next five thousand years.

Bear in mind that not everyone is compatible, either in business, or in love. Not everybody will love you, nor will you love everybody. It is alright to have differences with people. In business you will find that your business partner wants to do something different, or that the person is working at a different rhythm to you. Do not be square. Do not let your ego dominate you. Be nice. Be a team player. It is better to win as a team than as a solo founder. I think so. I know the Amazon guy was a solo founder. But, to be honest, you need business partners; someone that can keep you accountable. Same with life.

By the way, whenever you walk, walk like a king, or walk as if you do not give a damn about who the king is. They said it on Peaky Blinders. It matters. Walk straight, have good posture. Head up and never looking down. If you look at the floor you will get inside your mind. Getting inside your mind will create destructive and negative thoughts in most cases, or at least, trashy thoughts. When looking up, you will discover the world. You will see other people's faces and get more creative.

To finish this chapter about education, just get a degree. It does not matter if you were not the smartest guy in high school. Fuck those nerdy-narrow-minded-and-thin-skin-bastards that teachers loved who got all the A's. Wait, I love them too, they have also been my friends, and they are good employees. Cheers for those crazy guys, willing to do well at school but also having many friends and being good at sports.

Go to university, pay for it, aim for scholarships, but get a degree. You are way more likely to do well in life if you get educated. Do everything you can to get a master's afterwards and if possible, a PhD. No reason not to do it. Education and health are all you need to achieve everything in life. Knowledge is priceless. There are new worlds that you keep discovering. Study hard. Do not cheat on your exams. Learn for real. Your future self will thank you a lot.

Your children and grandchildren will love you more for that. If it is at a top school, even better. If you cannot make it to a top school, no problem, but at least try. You can go to Harvard if you try. The steps are filling and gathering very stressful documentation, taking some tests, and the last one is to be incredibly lucky. But we can all have a chance to go to Harvard (if you prepare yourself like an unstoppable beast of course). Stop thinking stuff in life is unreachable (Trump is president of the US!).

You are alive, you are beautiful, you are smart, and you have the winner mindset. A winning mindset equals a hard worker, an honest and ambitious person. Use all the knowledge for good. Have ethics. Have respect for other cultures. Never be a racist. We have the same brain and bones. Education makes you less racist, if you are already racist. Race does not matter. So if you are, you should not be. What matters is how fun, ambitious, smart, beautiful, whatever other things that come from the soul. Be open, be bold. Study a lot. It certainly decreases the risk of being dumb and stupid in life.

11. FINAL STATEMENT

Read one more page, do one more rep, write one more paragraph, become addicted to gains, run two more minutes, give it all. In this last rep is where winners and losers get separated. Build your happiness. Choose a life. Love your friends. Call them, talk to them. Do not be shy to answer the phone, or to do video calls with the ones you love. Be honest about your feelings. Do not give a damn about showing your fears and about being truthful to yourself. Be authentic. Do not copy other people. Girls will notice if you do. It does not play to your advantage. It is better to eat lunch with someone you like than alone. Eating alone is fine as long as you can notice and guide your mind to avoid negative thoughts.

Life is kind of a lonely journey. Most of the time you will be doing things by yourself. Before you get married and have kids of course. I enjoy being alone so much. There is no bullshit; it is just you, the real one. Whenever you are able to stand up and be yourself, the same self that you are while being alone, but with others, that day you win life. When people love you for who you are, you feel happy. When people tell you what your good characteristics are, you get happy. It has to come from a person you respect and appreciate. But anyway, you already have some traits that other people think are amazing. Bad things too, for sure. But we all learn constantly. We all change. We have to be able to embrace a new me. People who get stuck, actually get stuck. If you do not travel, dare to do what you want to do, or care too much about what other people say, you are going to live a miserable life.

Or maybe you like to live a normal life, nothing special. But even in a normal life, the kind of one of marriage, kids, stability and shit, if you are not yourself you will be feeling wounded forever. Life goes fast, so dare to take risks. Just honestly do not give a damn, everyone has shit they are ashamed of. Relax. Invest in yourself. It is freaking cool to care for oneself. Do not care if people think you are stupid or uncool because you really want to make it big in life. I just couldn't care less (I have done it, but honestly I don't now). Not even what my parents or my brother, or friends, told me. I do me, and I do not have to give explanations as long as I am not killing anyone or asking for money.

When you pick a path, you make your money, you take your own decisions, and people will respect you. Respect is something you work for. You want a salary raise? Cool bro, how much money are you going to bring to the company? If you bring a lot of money why will someone not pay you more for that? But you have to work. You cannot be the type of person that asks for things without showing why, in an objective way, you deserve them. Have common sense in life. But enjoy it. Just do that. Be thankful. This paragraph, and the next ones in this chapter are a fresh rain of good vibes. As I hope the book has been.

Our ego is soft with people that inspire us. We do not hate people that put us on the right track. As an example, a friend of mine from Sweden, who I met while I was living in Lisbon, told me after not seeing each other for two years, that I was his inspiration to start going to the gym. I didn't even know about it. Sometimes we do things and we share our experiences without knowing we will be an example for others. Sometimes also, we listen carefully to friends' stories or to other people's conversations and we get so excited that our life changes. It happens that it was also because of him that I decided to move to Sweden to study. He kept telling me about the advantages of studying in such a beautiful and developed country. Sweden is a country characterized by having a high level of honesty in its population. This allows the country to move forward more easily because people trust other people. The level of social trust is one of the highest in the world. I chose this path, now I am here.

I have been inspired by business stars, YouTubers, like the How to Beast channel, or friends. The more progress you make, the closer they feel to you. Suddenly, all the successful people become humans too, and you understood that what they made was just pure sacrifice. I was motivated to launch my own company when I was still studying at university. I let myself fall in love with the idea of having my own business. I was inspired, not by my dad or my mom (maybe indirectly by them), but by people I think I know are extremely successful. If you want to achieve big things in life you should get inspired by the right people. It would have been very easy for me to let myself be inspired by "cool" people in my hometown and get into drugs or hippie ways of life. That is not what I want in life. I may not know what I want, but I know what I do not want.

You have to enjoy every happy moment in life because in the future you will see how happy you were and you did not know it. It is a cliché to say that is important to remember. I kept thinking about myself growing older all the time and I can't stop thinking about what my child would look like. Am I going to get a wife I want to make love to every day of my life? Am I going to have cool friends? Am I going to have a good salary? Am I going to love my job? Where the fuck am I going to live? And then multiple questions related to this matter. But the thing is that life itself always finds a way to surprise us for good or for not so good.

When we push life, when we do shit and get out of our rooms and start talking to people to see what they think, is when we can see our potential in life. I compare myself many times with other people and I have not found anyone like me. They might look like me, be as funny as me, be as handsome as me, be with the girl I think I want to be, but they are just not me. I do know how I am and I do know my potential. This is extremely important. People out there are better than us in many other ways, but life is like that. Some unfair and fair advantages have come with us since we were born. I really would have liked to have a body shape that is V-shaped-naturally, or the swimmer's body type. But fuck it, I just went to the gym for two years and got the body I wanted. Those are the things that make us proud.

Again, always thinking in the long term. Always thinking about what would benefit me in ten years but doing what will be good for me now to achieve that. When I look at some old people and I see they have just a couple of friends, I just can't stand that. I want to get old with many friends. I want to keep discussing the world with them, and when we are older I want to know more about how they are dealing with aging. That would be so awesome. I want to do that. Therefore, I push myself to meet the people I know are going to be my friends in the future. Friends are something nice; some of them are in your life for just a couple of months and then they leave. A true friendship does not necessarily have to last forever. Friends can be there when you need them for some time and then the relationship is going to become less "enjoyable" because we are evolving people (to change friends is a good sign though).

We are not a static definition. We keep reinventing ourselves all the time. Our feelings and our desires that are very deep in us may remain for a long time, but in the day-to-day life we keep changing our mood and our thoughts. That is why meditation is just so important. It keeps you in the moment and lets you realize that you are changing all the time because you are just creating random thoughts all the time. You are not your thoughts, but all of the actions we take in life come from thoughts. To cultivate a positive and a right mindset towards life requires compromise, time and effort. It does not come for free. To have a healthy mind takes time, many years I would say. But it is worth it. A healthy mind leads to good relationships. We do not live alone. We live to provide happiness and sadness to other people. Everything is connected.

We are on a planet that we share. We share all of these common places. We live on planet Earth. We are all humans with dreams and regrets. Personally, I love women so much. I think they are just so beautiful and amazing; it makes me so happy when summer comes and they dress in skirts and light colors. And also it makes me very happy when in the winter they put on those serious black coats that make them look like they are working for some secret agency. Life is like that, life is beautiful. I love to see all of them and there is nothing wrong with that. I also like to see men dressed up in suits and in sports clothing. I just like seeing people caring about how they look. They all do. We all should do it, because it is important to show a good image to other people.

It is so easy to see when someone took the time to dress in a way to impact society or just because they had to put on something. Here comes the point I want to mention. It is: to put effort, again, to push life. We all have to push life in order to get the shit we want. Of course bad days will come and we will anguish but that also is part of life. But it is just so beautiful to see someone pushing and pushing to look more beautiful, to be more educated, to do better at business, to be a better parent, to be a better friend...etc. Life is the act of being alive, and that is related to the fact that we live on this planet for many days, and that we do not know most things. We have to get the experience we need to deal with shit, and then we learn. We are human beings, again, evolving all the time.

I do not know if most people relate to this, but I like the people that keep challenging themselves, and wishing and doing more than they should be doing. I love writing and I love studying. I love going to the gym. I know I might be in a good position now, but I want to be on another level. The next one. I just want to keep growing and be my better version. I am just not doing it for myself, I am doing this for my parents, my friends, the people I will meet in the future and of course, for my future wife. I know the girl I want to marry needs a man who is a motherfucker pushing life a lot who can give attention and lots of love to the children we will have. I have no rush. I keep listening to my music and growing. I like people building up the same mindset of growing all the time and I want to be around those people.

Today is the day after. I wrote those words in a state of pure joy. Yesterday I went out and sometimes I was like a motherfucker at the party and other times I was just feeling tired and not enjoying it that much. But like that, the moments of joy are not permanent, they are just small moments. They last for seconds. Maybe yesterday I got a smile from the girl working in the bar who is honestly like an angel, and I did ask her name, but by now I don't remember it. Yesterday I laughed and talked a lot of shit with people I am starting to consider my friends.

Now, I think I have been growing as a person. It is very challenging when you are trying to build up a network of friends of people that may be younger and stupid in my case, but at the same time they are the ones that I know are going to be cool and smart in the future. It is so easy to see the potential in people who might have a successful outstanding life and those who will have a normal one. So, again, going out at night to build up a network and to make friends and to have fun is very important. Being patient and consistent and being the person you always are is also very important. It takes time but it is worth it.

Life kicks us in the face all the time. I heard the other day that it is like a boxing fight: it doesn't matter how many punches in the face you can give, but how many you can resist. The one that can resist more is the one who will win the fight of life. And life keeps punching you all the time and it will never stop. There is beauty in that. It makes life amazing because if you put effort in and if you know where you are going in life, you can resist more and you are willing to be more patient. Control your mind; control who you want to be. You can do it bro!

Moreover, when you get a girlfriend at this age (before 35 years old I'd say), you gotta make sure you want to have sex with her all the time. Anthony Bourdain said: "Your body is not a temple, it's an amusement park. Enjoy the ride". Later, a partner will offer you more than that. At this moment, you do not get into a relationship because she is a good fit for your life. Sex is important. If you desire her all the time and you can be around other girls that are even prettier than her, but you still choose her over them because she is the type of girl you enjoy having sex with, then it is ok. It is alright. If she also has other attributes that you like, then why not give it a chance.

Sometimes we might start thinking that someone better will come along later and we do not take the chances we have now. It might be her, the girl you have been wanting for. Again, sex is very important, extremely important. However, man, the connection you get with her matters a lot too. You have to get excited about seeing her naked and also seeing her in the supermarket with clothes on. It is great to be with someone. I know it is not easy. Getting the right one is very hard. Mark Manson says you should make that one, the one. But I do not know; just when you focus on yourself everything will come. Getting girls should never be the goal of the night or of life. Improving oneself and making decent money is the goal.

Take care of your money. Spending a dollar on something you could avoid will put you a dollar further from your dreams. Just keeping the last random thoughts of the book, you can make people happy by giving them small presents. For example, if you organize a party and you give some of your guests, or all of them, a small present they will feel like you are a very generous and great person. Be that person that gives a small unexpected present.

Try to put yourself in the position of the giver more often than the receiver (it sounds sexual, but here I am talking about resources: time, work and money). Enjoy the benefits and the good energy of people who will consider you a very friendly and good person. Of course everything is in balance. Always try to keep everything balanced. But, take care of the money. Start a business, get rich. Just joking. Work hard, take risks, enjoy your life, have great sex, great friends and be a good human being.

I want to finish the book now for real, with an introduction to what the book of poems will be about. I am going to describe how I feel with my life in Sweden. It is a very hard country. People do not get much sun, therefore they are very shy. Social circles are closed, but they've got the cash and the beautiful girls (just joking, but they do actually). Also, they've got the innovation, the big companies, the dark winters and the great friends. It is not a country for everyone. But I will describe how it is to live in the biggest student town of Sweden.

EPILOGUE

When you love the place where you live, you do not even realize it. The small things we do not appreciate are the ones that we will miss the most if we change location in our life. In addition, there is no perfect place. Even Stockholm, which may be characterized for having a high standard of living, is not perfect. There is traffic and a busy metro every day. There are thousands of people with angry and stressful faces. And if you are alone in a perfect city you will find yourself caught in your own life lies. Happiness does not come from the outside. Definitely not. Of course, you need to live in a peaceful, developed and stable place. Those are the basics. But a city or a place with that standard of life is not going to dictate your happiness. I have friends living in Canada telling me how depressed they are because of the weather, the lack of friends and of course the lack of girls.

So it happens that none of these things come for free in life. Nothing worth it comes easy. So if you do not like your place and you think it is the place you live in that is making you go crazy or feel unsatisfied, you are wrong. You can't imagine how much social growth you could have only because of the fact that you speak the same language. Making friends consists of talking for the first time with someone you will see quite often. If you do not see people often, they will not be your friends. That is the reason why going to the gym is good too. Signing up to different classes of sales, biology, human rights, or whatever topic you are curious about helps you expand your network in the city. To love a city, is to love the friends you have in the city, and the girls you are sleeping with. You do not need much.

Living in Sweden has been a challenge for me, not only with girls, but with my patience and my anxiety. But to be honest, with all the ups and downs related to the weather and the culture, I am loving this place. I feel love. I am attached to it. I do not want to go now.

Hopefully you will find the continuation of this book useful for yourself, at least for entertainment. I have always liked the books that are kind of autobiographical. The ones that show the heart of the author. It will be a bit of that, with good content for keeping improving life, but as someone that comes to a new place and has the motivation to start a life from scratch.

I do follow my own advice in this book, but even if you are a perfect human being, you cannot control everything. Sometimes I still fuck it up. I keep failing. I forget stuff. I learn again. It is the normal course of life. It is like when you hate yourself after seeing a beautiful girl at the beach, and not talking to her. You know you have an opportunity: you are in the right place at the right time. You don't talk to her because you pussy out. Suddenly she leaves, and boom! You hit yourself mentally. Why the fuck am I never going to learn this shit? No risk, no gains. A winner mindset is composed of the attitude to be willing to take shit, i.e. failure or pain.

You increase the chances of getting better results in life and eventually fine things will come. But those roses do not come without some thorns. Sweden is a top country, no doubt. But as any other place in the world, it can be super boring and depressing. The good mood comes from the inside. I will tell you more about that. This book was the brain, the action and the practicalities. The next one is about the realities, the feelings, the mistakes, the lows, the highs, my identity, my honest view of the world and my way of being grateful with Sweden for giving me the chance to develop myself mentally, emotionally and physically.

Sending good vibes and much love. Improve the world, and take care of yourself. Don't forget to read Losing My Swedish Virginity II - Practical Poetry For a New Life. It is important to read it, because when those low moments come, you will know you are not alone.

Losing my

SWEDISH VIRGINITY II

Practical poetry for a new life

CÉSAR SUÁREZ

SKONVIK

ABOUT THE AUTHOR

César is a doer and a dreamer.

He knows what good literature looks like. He knows you need to taste life to be able to write about it.

He is an engineer and a guy with an economics background. Also, he is a Master from de department of Economic History from Lund University.

He is interested into discovering how the world works and how the human mind and feeling guide us in our actions. He is 70% and 30% fun.

Cesar loves to see and experience beauty, to see and exploit the potential of the human brain, to find the brightest minds and to work hard to become one and also, he loves to explore the world.

He wants to improve humanity. He keeps looking for ways to do it. Either through innovations or by writing.

———

If you want to contact him send an email to cesarlmsv@gmail.com and follow him on Instagram: @cesarsuarezpab

Don't forget to visit www.losingmyswedishvirginity.com